Steps and Corners

A Collection of Stories, Reminiscences, and Poems

by Jean Barringer

"Steps and Corners," by Jean Barringer. ISBN 978-1-62137-994-2 (softcover).

Published 2017 by Virtualbookworm.com Publishing Inc., P.O. Box 9949, College Station, TX, 77842, US.

Table of Contents

Introduction

This is a collection of little stories and poems.

I happen to have a phenomenal memory for detail and color and surroundings and things that have happened to me from the age of three.

Everything I remember is here, the good, the bad, the twists and turns. The mistakes I made and what happened as a result.

My story is about growing up in war-torn London, experiencing the air raids and hardships that go with fighting a war at home.

There aren't many of us left who remember as much as I do, and so that is why I feel it is very important to write it all down. World War II had a profound effect upon my life, as it did on all of us who were there.

Nothing is taken for granted, food is never wasted, and leftovers used to make another meal, clothing is mended to last a while longer, and socks darned, and I find I can't bring myself to buy anything I don't really need.

So this is about what it was like to be an ordinary young girl amongst thousands of other young people, all of us living in day-to-day situations, never looking far ahead, never planning a future because we didn't know whether there would be one.

At the age of ninety, I have decided that my life, with all its steps and corners, has turned into a very rich soup.

This then is my story.

– Jean Barringer

With acknowledgments to Carolyn Evans Campbell, whose creative writing classes started me on my writing adventure. The friends we made at her classes, writers themselves, Peggy Markham, Barrie Fiedler, Paula Bard, Catharine Bond – all of whom encouraged me. Countless others who listened, my daughter, Elisabeth, and daughter-in-law, Julie Barringer, for all their support and encouragement, and to Kerry Griess of Naxos Design for the typing and constant corrections made during the assembling of this book.

Thanks to all of you.

The Room

I sat in the window
watching the rain rivers
coursing down the glass
meeting and merging.

A little girl of three, nearly four
alone in the living room
of the old dark Victorian flat
where I was born.

Across the road
the railway yards
where the wagons emptied coal
into the horse-drawn carts.

The air thick with coal dust,
the half curtains
in the window where I sat,
tasting of soot.

I heard the cracked voice
of the singing man
as he stood in the rain
begging for pennies.

I cried a lot for the singing man
outside in the wet
splashed by the coal carts
as they went by.

Behind me, a low fire
sputtered in the grate, without warmth.
Vines twisted and turned
on the tiles around
the little Victorian fireplace.

Roses climbed on trellises
up the wall to the ceiling
and there was an
oval cornice in the middle
that looked like an airship.

Two gas lamps sat on brass brackets
one each side of the fireplace,
popped when they were lit
and hissed with a cold greenish glow.

I remember how quiet
it was in that room.
I was a lonely little girl
with no one to play with
and nothing to do.

And then my Daddy came home.
He showed me how
to spell my name
and draw pictures,
to read the big billboards
outside the window –
Oxo, Bovril and Pears Soap.

He taught me my ABCs
and to count to 100,
and showed me how to play
"Mary Had a Little Lamb"
with one finger
on my toy piano.

Then that room came alive
with the warmth of his voice
and the stories he read to me
about fairies and giants
and dancing princesses,
feeding my young mind
so ready and eager to learn.

The Singing Man

It was a cold wet afternoon, my mother held my hand as we made our way along the busy street of our town. Great steaming dray horses pulling carts of coal plunged by, smelling of horse-sweat and manure, splashing through puddles, sending showers of muddy water into the air, and soaking the man who stood at the edge of the pavement.

An old World War I overcoat, dirty and frayed, hung on his thin frame. His grey hair, long and unkempt lay over his collar as he stood in the rain. He sang, in a high thin faltering voice "It's a long way to Tipperary, it's a long way to go"...His cap lay on the ground in front of him, empty except for a few pennies.

I clung to my mother's hand as she hurried past, I pulled, and turned to look, "Mommy wait, a penny for the man" but she walked quickly past without glancing. "Don't stare" she said "it's rude". "But Mommy" I pleaded. There was no answer.

Other women, shopping baskets over their arms also hurried by, although a few paused long enough to drop a penny into his sodden cap, receiving a nod of thanks.

We passed other ex-soldiers, selling matches, or pencils, grey faced and gaunt.

It was 1930, I was four years old.

I never forgot those men, and the indifference of the women who passed them by, or crossed over onto the other side of the street to avoid their pleading eyes.

Epilogue

A short time later as my parents and I sat at the supper table, my father said in a jovial voice "Well if I lose my job I can always sing in the street".

I was seized with terror remembering the singing man, and knew that my father couldn't sing at all. He wouldn't get any pennies in his hat.

This just shows you that you have to be very careful what you say in front of a four-year-old child.

Visit to my Godmother

The long, dark staircase
steep, climbing forever
for short stubby legs.

The room
filled with stuffed birds
in glass cases
glittery glass eyes
seeing nothing.

Musty, dusty, mildewed curtains
dark red, and half pulled
against the light.

Ancient, stilled photographs
of long-dead who-knows-who.
Grey cat, grey windows
grey corners.
Grey-bearded grandpa
sitting quietly, watching.
Grey dust filling my nostrils.

Oppressive, cloying scent of time
long gone
Stilted, monotonous talk, smothering.

Down the long staircase once again
feeling under my small fingers
the brown embossed wall.

Out through the heavy door
Out into the living sunshine
The golden sparkling
light of life.

The Ballgown

She took the dress from where it lay
        and slipped it over her head.
It showed her shoulders
        nipped her tiny waist,
And fell in pink and silky folds
        around her feet.

She was nineteen
        my sweet Scottish aunt,
And I was three.

She let me brush her hair
        until it shone.
Then took a rose from her corsage
        and put it in my hands.

Now I am Four

I was four years old that day in April 1930, when I decided it was time to go to school. Harry, who lived next door went to school and so I knew where to go, and how to get there.

I knew my ABCs and how to count, and I could spell Oxo, and Bovril and Pears Soap from the big billboards outside on the street. My Daddy had taught me to spell and write my name and I wanted to learn more, I wanted to go to school.

I carefully packed my little school bag with a writing book and a pencil, and let myself out the front door. I didn't say "goodbye" to my mother, I knew she would have stopped me, so I was very quiet, like a mouse.

Down the outside stairs I went softly, softly, and out the garden gate. Nobody saw me as I walked along the quiet road that led to the town.

The town main street was busy with people and cars coming and going. I had to cross that crowded street, so I waited until a nice-looking lady came along, then asked her "Will you please see me across the road?"

I often think to myself now at this great age, how could anyone in their right mind, when they saw a very small girl all alone in the middle of a busy town, take her hand and see her across the road?

But this person did just that and I made my way to the school building about half a mile away.

The children were all out at recess, and I simply joined in. When the teacher came out with a big bell I went in with all the others and stood in line outside the classroom.

Then the teacher found me! A strange little girl clutching a school bag, I followed the other children into the classroom and sat down at a desk, opened my bag, got out my book and pencil and waited.

The teacher loomed in front of me "What's your name?" she asked. "Well, I'm Jeannie" I remember saying. "I'm four now, and I've come to school to learn."

She told me to draw a picture in my book, which I did; but I remember thinking, "Well I can draw pictures at home. This isn't learning." I told the teacher about my ABCs and how I could spell Oxo and Bovril and I wanted to learn. "That's why I came" I said again. "Harry comes to school, why can't I?"

I think the teacher must have sent for the principal at that point, because soon the principal came into the room, and with her was Harry. "Who's this?" she asked Harry, and Harry gave the game away, "It's Jeannie" he said.

But I was allowed to stay at school for the rest of that blissful afternoon and my mother was at the gate to meet me.

How she and my father explained to me I couldn't go back to school the next day, I don't know. It was another two years before I was able to go to school, a different school, a devastatingly different experience that took me down a very different path. The desire to learn, crushed right from the beginning.

My Geese

I sit in the warm sun watching a flock of geese fly by, and with feet outstretched before them, land on the water calling to each other.

My mind goes back to the time when I was four years old, standing beside my mother clutching a bag of bread for the geese in the park.

I loved the geese. I loved their soft grey feathers and bright black eyes, and their clean yellow bills. My geese also called, and I knew they were calling to me as they swam towards where I was standing.

My mother retreated as they got close and waded out onto the bank of grass. My mother was afraid of the geese, she said they could be very fierce, but I wasn't afraid.

The geese crowded around me, their long necks towering above my head.

I opened the bag and took the pieces of bread and held them out, and one by one the geese bent their heads and gently took the bread from my small fingers.

I stretched my hands towards them and they let me stroke their grey feathers.

My geese could not fly away like these Canada Geese in front of me, their wings were clipped. They lived their whole lives in a park pond waiting for the little girl with the blond curls who came every day to feed them.

Nobody's Birthday

"It's my birthday" I whispered to myself
full of anticipated joy.
At breakfast I waited.
Nobody said a word.

In the end I asked my mother
"Is there anything for me?"
"No" she said "why would there be?"
Nobody heard.

"It's my birthday" I whispered quietly to myself.
Nobody remembered.
Outside the house my tears ran unchecked.
Nobody noticed.

Grandmother's Magicky Attic

Steep and narrow slappity stairs
led to it.
A low door, even we as children
bent to enter.
A skylight, dusty and yellowed
with spidery webs and dead flies
barely lit it.
But our Grandmother's attic
lured my sister and me, it did,
to a magicky world.

We clambered up those slappity stairs
opened the tiny door
and entered the magicky attic.
Great trunks sat waiting
and with a squeaking and creaking
of hinges,
we slowly opened the lids, we did.

And there lay old clothes from long ago
carefully wrapped in tissue
with mothballs tucked into the folds.
Dresses with bustles,
tiny pilly-box hats,
tight waisted jackets, dark red
with black frogs
and braided buttons.

My Grandfather's clackity rocking chair
moved gently, all by itself.
Boxes of birds eggs packed in cotton,
collected by my father
as a boy.
A brass helmet from World War I,
worn by Uncle Jamie
"Royal Horse Artillery".
Our drawings, Doris's and mine,
flattened under mats
on the floor.
Children's books from time gone by.
China dolls with pursed lips
and glarey eyes,
loose arms and legs and tattered hair.

We put on the old dresses, we did,
worn long ago
by a great-great aunt,
paraded around the attic we did,
trailing skirts.
Dust flew, and moth balls rolled
across the floor.
We sat in the clackity rockity chair
and read the much loved books, we did.

Then hearing a call from down below
"Come awa' bairns"
We carefully folded the long-ago dresses,
wrapped them in tissue
once more, we did,
put them in the trunks
and closed the squeaky, creaky lids.
Then blissfully happy
and covered with dust,
down the slappity stairs we went
to an ordinary, everyday
dust-free world we went,
for afternoon tea.

The Beginning and The End

My school days were not the happy period of my childhood that they should have been.

In 1931 when I was 5, and my baby sister 18 months old, my father, a moody, hot tempered Scot, walked out of his job because of a clash with his boss over ideas, and because he couldn't have his own way.

This in the uncertain days of the depression, and with 2 young children to support. He was a pharmacist, and determined to be his own boss, and to open his own Pharmacy.

And so, we had to leave our home and go to live in a small flat in a different district in the rapidly growing suburb of London.

When I reached the age of 6, it came time for me to start school. We lived right on the edge of a poor, working-class neighborhood. There was no choice, there were no other schools.

My mother took me, that first day to the large, grim, grey Victorian building with a bell tower on the roof, up the stone steps, through the echoing corridors, to the Headmistress's office.

It was Easter, and so I was a new child entering a world that had already begun in September. The teacher, a tall, grey-haired lady in a blue dress, came and took me by the hand to the classroom where I stood alone confronted by the hostile stares of 30 children.

Right then I knew, even at the tender age of 6 that my life was not going to be easy. I was perhaps, a little better dressed than most of these children who were used to poverty and rough living and they labeled me.

I was given a desk in the front row, a worn, scratched desk with an inkwell and a shelf underneath for books.

The room was painted dark green on the bottom half and dirty cream above. There was a picture of "The Light of the World" which I didn't like, it scared me. There was a fireplace with a guard in front and a tall scuttle of coal and every so often the janitor would come and empty a few lumps onto the low smoking fire which gave out no heat at all. The room was lit by a large single gas light which sputtered and hissed and there was a smell of unwashed bodies and dirty hair.

The children were pale and thin, some of them had leg-irons, presumably from rickets, most had torn clothes, with sleeves too short, showing thin wrists.

I sat quietly at my desk waiting, while behind me the sounds of giggling and whispering was silenced by the teacher with a sharp slap of her ruler against her desk.

"Stand" she said "hands together, eyes closed". The garbled drone of "The Lord's Prayer" began and I remembered with terror being taken by my grandmother to her very austere Chapel the year before and being frightened beyond belief.

Panic swept over me and I screamed. The teacher stood over me, lifted me to my feet and shook me violently until I stopped while the children laughed uncontrollably.

It was a nightmare. I couldn't get out. At recess the children stood around me with poking, prodding fingers, saying words I had never heard before, but knew instinctively were bad. Nobody came to help.

Those days were my introduction to school.

After a time though, it got better. I learned to hold my head high, never to cry to betray my feelings of hurt, and amazingly to find ways to understand these children with their rough ways and coarse speech, and eventually to make friends with them.

Later in life I realized the value of that tough beginning and how it would enable me to accept people for who they are and not from what they appear to be.

Witch in the House

I have a sister
    you must know
Four years younger than I
    she is
And when we were young
    I hated her,
so I became a witch
    I did.
I thought of things
    that I could do
to make her life
    a misery.

At night when we were both
    in bed
I told her
    God was in the room
He had big hollow eyes
    I said
that glittered
    as he looked at her
She screamed
    she did
and I just laughed
    a high-pitched
cackling laugh
    and thought up
more ungodly pranks.

One night I went up early
    and climbed into the wardrobe
Yes I did
    and then I watched
her through a crack
    as she undressed
and went to bed
    I waited
until all was quiet
    Slowly then
I pushed the door
    and as it opened
creaked and squeaked
    and whined
        it did.

Then I appeared
and shone a light
    under my chin
and made a dreadful
    evil-looking mask
and groaned
    I did.

My sister yelled with fright
    she did
leaped out of bed
    And tore downstairs
while I remained
    convulsed - I did
        until my parents came!

I got the biggest walloping
    I did.
And after that, I had to keep
    my manic jokes
To quieter evil things.

But do you know
    I like her now
and strangely
    she likes me
        she does!

The May Dancer

It was my day.

        I was the leader.

The dancer, the May Day dancer.

        The maypole stood resplendent

bright ribbons hanging–waiting for the dancers' hands.

        I had never been a leader

Now it was my day.

Full of joy I danced home to get my dress.

        Pink it was soft and satiny. A dancer's dress.

Full of joy I turned to let my mother

        button it.

She raised my hair, and saw the telltale spots,

        "Measles" she said "you cannot go".

And the ribbons of my happiness

        were turned to rags.

The Secret Place

I had a secret place
       where I would go
a quiet protected space
       where no one came.

I had three uncles
       my mother's brothers
not much older than I
       who took delight
          in teasing me
       to make me cry.

I had a shell
       against the taunts
the jeers and sneers
       and learned
to hold my head
       up high
To smile and not to show
       the hurt
never to cry to show
       the hurt.

I had my secret place
       where I would go
but never forgot
       the cruel jibes
And because of that sad
       abused child
my children never knew
       such taunts
that pushed them
       to a point of despair
or needed a secret place.

Beginnings and Endings

It was always cold in the house where I grew up. A small suburban home north of London, in a row of other homes, all joined together and all the same. They were neat, tidy, and respectable.

These were first homes for most people, young, in their 30's. Most Dads had been in World War I, none of them wealthy, struggling in a tight economy, to make a living. Most families consisted of one or maybe two children, never more.

None of us had cars, we traveled everywhere by bus or train, which meant a lot of waiting at cold draughty bus stops or train stations.

Inside each identical house was a kitchen, a living-dining room, and a front room, called the "drawing room". This room was never used. It smelled of dust and mildew, had the best furniture, and was kept for visitors and special occasions, like Christmas. Upstairs were three bedrooms and a bathroom.

My family lived in the kitchen and living room. We ate there, sat there, listened to the radio there and did our homework there. The room had brown pattern wallpaper, the chairs were brown too, and over the dining room table hung a lamp enclosed in a bowl-like fixture, frosted glass with orange streaks, which gave out very little light. This in fact was the only light; there were no table lamps in those days. There was a little coal fire, which was the only source of warmth in the whole house.

We huddled around it in the winter, and the fronts of the legs became mottled with the heat from the fire, while our backs froze.

My mother always had a little window open "because," she said, "I like my house to be airy." But the draught whistled through and down across the floor, and up the chimney.

My feet were always cold, so were my hands.

When we left that room to go to bed we entered another world. Out there it was so cold, I remember an icicle hanging from the bathroom faucet all winter, the pipes always froze, and of course there was no hot water. We had baths once a week in the kitchen using a tin bathtub which hung on a nail outside the back door for the rest of the week.

My sister and I undressed in our icy bedroom, and took our clothes into bed with us, and in the morning we dressed under the blankets.

Everybody I knew lived this way; we didn't complain, it was normal. We all had chilblains which is a form of frost bite. Our fingers, toes and heels became red and inflamed and swelled, then itched and burned and finally broke and bled. I remember not being able to hold a pencil at school, my joints were so swollen.

In a strange kind of way, I think the British were proud of being able to survive and withstand these severe conditions.

I didn't know any difference until years later when my husband and I emigrated to

Canada, and I lived for a week with a friend in her apartment in Montreal. It was warm, every room was warm, all the doors were open and it was still warm. I couldn't believe it!

I arrived in February, the coldest month. Outside below zero, inside we wore cotton shirts and short sleeves. My chilblains disappeared in two days and have never returned. Wonder of wonders!

However, even now, as a legacy of those cold British years, my hands are always cold when I'm outside in the winter, no matter how warm my gloves are.

Thankfully, the British overcame their desire to be martyrs, and now have their homes installed with central heating and hot water heaters, but it has only been within the last few years. So tourists beware, take along your woolens, just in case!

The Mystery of the Lost Will

There is a story in my family of a will with a missing page, and wealth gone astray. Of a great-great-grandmother Isabella Keith, who was somehow related to the Earls of Keith in Northern Scotland.

So enticing was this story that my sister and 1 would spend hours romanticizing about finding the lost page in an old trunk in my grandmother's attic. Indeed there were a lot of old trunks in that attic, and many a rainy day was spent unearthing old treasures, because our grandmother never threw anything away.

But we never found the lost page that could have entitled us to millions of pounds, and proof that we were Lady Jean and Lady Doris.

However, the story persisted, and an aunt even went so far as to trace the family history, in the days before computers. She went to London, to Somerset House where there were records of every family in the land, and a document was made.

It showed that amazingly we could trace our ancestry back to the ancient Kings of Scotland, and then to the great Earls Marischal, the Earls of Keith.

So one day when my daughter was in High School, she had a project to do on Family History. We unearthed the old documents and proceeded to make a family tree on a very, very long scroll of paper.

We started at the beginning and it went on and on through the ages, until at the very end we came to our great-great-grandmother Isabella Keith, daughter of the last Earl Marischal of Scotland, who died at the age of 80 - unmarried!

The Backway

Between my childhood years of 5 and 11, my family lived in a modest suburb of London in a street of look-alike houses, each with a small front garden with a low wall, and a gate, facing another row of look-alike homes across the road.

There was a fair-sized yard at the back with a concrete patio, grass and flower beds, and a garage for our recently acquired and much prized Ford 8, bright blue and named "Bluebell".

Beyond the back fence was the Backway. It was an unpaved road between our row of fences and the fences of our neighbors on the next street over.

The Backway was rutted, and weeds grew at the sides lush and unkempt, and it was where the neighborhood children played, unwatched and unsupervised. It was heaven!

During a rain, the ruts became muddy puddles leading one to another like rivers and lakes. We made boats out of matchboxes and sails out of toothpicks and pieces of notepaper, and sailed them through banks and cliffs of mud and sand to a land of make-believe.

One boring day when there had been no rain and everything was dry and dusty, we moped around wondering what to do and found ourselves outside a vacant house with the garage facing the backway, the door fastened from the inside with a wooden bar. We discovered that a stick poked through the crack could lift the bar, and the door swung open.

Inside was all kinds of junk the previous owner had left behind. A worn down broom, some rope, an old cauldron, wooden planks and buckets and a terrible smell of garbage left in a pile in a side room.

Our young minds went to work. We could make this into a clubhouse. We wouldn't tell our parents, or anyone else; it would be a secret hiding place.

And so it became, that summer of 1936. The neighborhood kids were all involved, and sworn to secrecy with pretend blood smeared on the backs of our hands.

We swept it clean, put planks on upturned buckets and had secret meetings, elected a president, a secretary, messengers, cleaners, and lookouts for grown-ups walking their dogs down the Backway, whereupon we would close the doors and remain very quiet until the coast was clear.

For some strange reason, nobody inquired where we were, or came looking for us.

All went well that glorious summer, until one member had the brilliant idea of lighting a fire in the cauldron and cooking sausages on sticks held over the fire.

The smell of those sausages wafted through the neighborhood and a woman noticed smoke coming under the doors and called the fire department who arrived with bells clanging and hoses at the ready. They burst through the doors to find all of us sitting in the smoke eating sausages.

And I'm afraid that was the end of our Backway hideaway.

British Christmas

I awoke in the half-light of Christmas mornings, those years as a child, with a weight on my feet at the end of the bed where my presents were stacked all unwrapped. I don't think people wrapped presents in those days.

Doris and I spent a frenzied hour gloating over the mostly books and games we received from aunts and uncles and grandparents, always the religious books from my mother's mother.

From downstairs came the clinking of dishes, the footsteps to-ing and fro-ing and the whistle of the tea kettle proclaiming breakfast.

My mother always made a special effort at Christmas. There was a crackling fire in the fireplace, and the table laid with a white cloth. Ham and eggs and the smell of crusty fresh bread with butter and marmalade.

Afterwards we went out into the frosty air for a walk. I don't remember snow ever, but hoar frost coated the trees and when the sun shone through the branches, everything glistened with tiny rainbows.

We came home to hot chocolate and scones baked on the griddle and served with butter and strawberry jam.

The scent of roasting chicken (we never had turkey) with stuffing. The plum pudding simmering in the pot of boiling water, the top of the pudding bowl wrapped in a cloth with a knot on top. We never had a tree, "too messy" my mother said, "'too much work, all those pine needles all over the floor".

Christmas dinner was eaten around one o'clock and after our walk in the cold air we were hungry. My mother had been cooking all morning, alone, because she never wanted anyone in the kitchen with her. I understand this now, I like to be on my own too, when I'm cooking.

So when we sat down to eat, it was with a hot and weary cook, but we made sure we voiced our appreciation of all the effort she had made.

The brown, crusty-skinned chicken, the roast potatoes and parsnips (try them) and slightly crisp Brussells sprouts, gravy made from scratch never packaged. We barely had room for plum pudding, but we made room because there's nothing like Christmas pudding! What would Christmas be without it?

Not surprisingly, my Mom and Dad needed a nap after all that eating and so Doris and I washed the dishes and put them away.

Would you believe that at five o'clock we sat down to Christmas tea? Tea is a meal in Britain, not just a drink, and in this case little hot mince pies and Christmas cake (always a high round fruit cake decorated with marzipan and white icing) and trifle.

Now, English fruit cake is not to be confused with American fruit cake, which l understand is a bit of a joke. English fruit cake is made with small fruit, not large fruit glued together with cake.

English fruit cake is rich and moist made of course with butter, raisins, golden raisins, currants, peel, chopped nuts and when baked (which takes three to four hours) and while still warm, brandy is poured over the bottom and allowed to soak in. I may add that this glorious cake has to be made 3 months ahead and allowed to mature.

There is always a silver sixpence wrapped in tissue paper hidden in the cake and whoever finds the sixpence in their slice has luck all year.

Satiated and heavy with food, we dragged ourselves from the table.

Remembering those Christmasses before the war when there were no shortages and no rationing, the day punctuated by food, I doubt I could eat half of it nowadays.

So our British Christmasses were not about presents, we didn't have that many, they were more like the American Thanksgiving with the emphasis on getting together and enjoying delicious food.

And despite the bad reputation British cooking has, I can assure you that properly prepared, it is wonderful. Unadulterated by garlic and spices, you can taste the vegetables and fruit just the way they are meant to taste. So I ignore the amused taunts of my friends and cook the British way.

The Wall

The Church of St. Lawrence sits in the middle of the town of Forres in the north of Scotland. Surrounding it is an ancient stone wall, and from the crevices grow tiny ferns and alpine plants such as sedum, rockcress, lichen and moss.

As a girl I used to trail my hand over the rough granite and smell the sweet, warm scent of growing things, climb the steps and wander through the church yard with the leaning grave stones, old and undecipherable. At one point the wall takes a right angle turn and becomes the side of my grandmother's house with one window built into the side of it.

Nowadays a saddler's shop occupies the lower level but I am told that long ago this was the Bishop's house and must have been rather grand. You have to pass through an archway into the cobbled close (alley) to reach the front door. Having once been the Bishop's house would explain the large double front door which still displays the brass fixtures, a door knocker, letter box and door knob so very different from the modest little houses lining the rest of the close. And inside, why there is a wide, curved staircase with its carved banisters leading to the upper floors.

This house was where we came to from London each summer to visit our Granny and our two Aunts, Bess and Kate who lived at home.

Upstairs, the large living room overlooked the High Street; the windows set deep into the thick walls with window seats and blue wooden shutters closed at dusk against the night.

The oil lamps were lit (electricity was late getting to Forres), and one lamp was placed in the center of the round table which was set for High Tea, a lovely light supper meal we all loved.

After the dishes were cleared away we would gather around the table and by the lamp's gentle light, Doris and I would read and the aunts would knit or embroider or sometimes we played cards.

Bedtime meant climbing the stairs by candlelight to the attic bedrooms we shared with the two aunts.

The little side room with the window in the wall became Granny's kitchen, but maybe at one time, long ago, it was the Bishop's study. Perhaps he would look out and see the great spire of his church and the wall surrounding it. Then on Sundays on his way to the church he would make his way down the curving staircase holding onto the same carved banister rail Doris and I did two hundred years later.

I expect he would step carefully over the threshold of the same big front door and then pass under the archway at the head of the close onto the High Street. I like to think that the Bishop also touched the stones of the old wall, feeling the rough granite beneath his hands, and breathing the same warm sweet scent of growing things.

The Lost Garden

Long ago,
        I, a child then,
Climbed into the raspberry canes to pick.
        A white enamelled bucket in my hands.

The berries hung like crimson drops,
        So ripe, they plopped into the bucket by themselves.

A long abandoned garden.
        The walls of the cottage peering from the grass.
Reproachful grey stone eyes.

But oh, the warm scented berries,
        wasted if we didn't take them,
Lost and squashed in the damp dark earth
        beneath the canes.

The Way Things Were

Pat McKenzie's hardware store stood in the High Street facing the bank on the opposite side of the street.

Forres was a market town. Farmers came to town and visited the hardware store for all their agricultural needs; it was a very busy place.

Granny would send me on errands and I loved going to Pat McKenzie's hardware store for her kitchen candles, bar soap for laundry and clothes pegs.

Over the years Mr. McKenzie was joined by Mr. Cruickshank and the name over the door was re-painted in gold on green, "McKenzie and Cruickshank". But it was still the same fascinating store, smelling pungently of creosote and old rope. The floorboards still creaked and they still sold nuts and bolts and screws, little brass hooks and hasps, hammers and saws and screwdrivers of all shapes and sizes.

Mr. McKenzie was tall and broad and bristled with a curly red beard, eyebrows that stuck out over twinkly blue eyes, while Mr. Cruickshank was short and dumpy and bald. He wore steel-framed glasses and had jowls that wobbled when he spoke or laughed.

Both gentlemen wore brown aprons with large capacious pockets, each divided into smaller, narrower pockets out of which protruded wooden folding rulers, scissors and notebooks. Each of them had pencils lodged behind their ears, as carpenters do, and both gentlemen knew how to fix everything.

In my grandmother's day you could buy oil lamps embellished with roses and violets and of course lamp oil, fancy chamber pots, candlesticks with handles on the sides and saucers to catch the wax because then, we all went to bed by candlelight.

They sold bellows to hang by the fireplace. On the wall hung washboards and below them trays of Sunlight Soap. There were copper sticks for lifting hot laundry out of the copper to put through the mangle. They sold mangles too and flat irons and trivets. All kinds of necessary items came from McKenzie and Cruickshank's Hardware Store and I loved going in and smelling the "hardwarey" smells.

Farmers gathered there on market day to discuss the weather and the state of the crops that year, all of them weather beaten with wind burned faces and big Scottish noses. All Scotsmen seem to have big noses.

Other farmers kept sheep or cattle and all had border collies to help bring the livestock down from the hills and all the dogs had fleas and scratched themselves constantly. Market day was particularly busy for the farmers, they were everywhere on the High Street bringing their wives who did their shopping and met other wives and stood in groups gossiping.

Those were lovely days, but after World War II things changed. My sister tells me McKenzie and Cruickshank is still there although Mr. McKenzie and Mr. Cruickshank are long gone. The oil lamps are gone too, so are the candlesticks and kitchen candles. Nobody washes on a washboard now or uses Sunlight Soap.

Electric devices have replaced them and it's a different less interesting store. You can still buy gardening tools and there is a pervasive smell of fertilizers sold in big plastic bags. A lot of "gifty things" for sale but the floor boards still creak "although they are replacing them with vinyl squares", my sister says.

When I came to Evergreen forty years ago I was astonished to find the same hardware store I left behind in Scotland also smelling of creosote and old rope and where you could buy one screw if you wanted it and it would be put into the same little brown paper bag. It also had the same creaky floor boards and wooden staircase. It was one of my favorite places to go.

Sad, sad when it closed. Didn't they realize what a gold mine they had?

I know things change, sometimes for the better, sometime not. But I think it's important for we who remember, to write it down so that those who come after us will know the way things were.

The Front Room

In my childhood days
I lived in a row
of look-alike homes.
Each with a Front Room
that was never used.

Our "'Front Room"
was cold and bare.
Best furniture
smelling of mildew
sat there unused.

Every day
I practiced piano
with fingers so numb
they hardly moved.
The door was closed
on our "Front Room",
nobody graced
that wasted space.

Maureen lived
two homes away,
the door open
on her Front Room.
Inside we danced
and sang,
played that old piano
'til it rocked.

Pushed back the chairs,
danced like
Fred and Ginger
Micky and Judy
Shirley Temple.
We left the windows bare
just in case
a film director
passed that way,
seeing the vast talent
through the window
of that Front Room,
signed us up
on the spot
for a screen test.
Saw the amazement
of our families,
that their two girls
were future movie stars.
All seen through
the windows
of their own Front Room.

Grandmother's Story

Brown-apple lined face, black hair parted in the middle, drawn back into an untidy knot. No time to comb or braid it properly, no time to wash it.

Family to feed, no time for herself. Hands worn into knobby claws, rough and calloused, hardened by work and the cleaning of the cookstove with black lead polish. Knees worn by kneeling to scrub floors muddied permanently by many boots.

But saved by her intense love of her church and the support of the women in "The Peculiar People's Chapel" where she went for peace and to be alone just for an hour or two on Sundays. This lady was my grandmother when I knew her as a child.

But it wasn't always that way. She grew to young womanhood as Anna Ellis, the daughter of a prosperous farmer, who was also head-gamekeeper to King Edward VII.

Anna was pampered, and wanted for nothing in that large stone farmhouse in Norfolk County on the East Coast of England. She had a glowing olive skin, sparkling eyes, and long black curling hair, and oh how she loved to dance!

At 16, she met a young man, blond with blue eyes and a curling moustache who regaled her with stories of an adventurous life full of bravery and heroism, and to which, naive and innocent as she was, she believed, and fell totally in love.

They were married, much against her parents' wishes. They probably eloped, headstrong as she was.

Then she found out, much too late, that my grandfather's tales of heroism were all fabricated. His family was very poor, and she came to her marriage with a trunkful of beautiful clothes which were immediately seized and distributed amongst her new in-laws.

The babies came one after another, fourteen in all, and by the age of 40 she was an old woman.

But Anna was strong and resilient and reared all her children to be healthy and strong men and women. Some dark with flashing eyes like herself, or tall and blond with a "gift of the gab," like my grandfather.

Later in life though, Anna became quite a gal. She wore stylish dresses, and fashionable hats, and traveled frequently to London to visit us. She would sit listening to our stories and adventures with a quiet smile, thinking no doubt that there was a bit of our grandfather in us all.

The Empty Shell

My mother grew up as second eldest in a family of 14. My grandfather was strict, as no doubt he had to be, and didn't "spare the rod".

Obviously there wasn't much room for love in that large rambunctious family, so I feel she faced life not really knowing what it meant.

Her cousin found her a job as a lady's maid in a large wealthy household, and it was there she learned to appreciate fine clothes and acquired the excellent taste which she had the whole of her life.

She was a small woman, attractive, with clear brown eyes, a creamy skin, and long shining nut-brown hair, which she twisted into a knot. She stood erect, and appeared taller than 5 '2" because of her high-heeled shoes.

The day she met my father, a college-educated man, she determined that when she married, it would be to "better herself" and she saw in my father a life that would lift her out of drudgery.

I was born and four years later my sister, but she had no patience for babies, what she wanted were dolls to bend to her will, dress up and show off, she didn't bargain for a couple of strong-willed little girls.

And so she, like her father before her did not "spare the rod", and Doris and I were the recipients of punishments in the form of smackings dealt with a wet hand, and as I heard her say once, "because it leaves the mark of my hand – and stings more".

Not once did she give us hugs, or kiss us good-night, or give us the encouragement and praise we craved. She simply didn't know how. Sadly, she had other cruel streaks which deprived her of any friends she had. She would criticize those women behind their backs, which of course got back to them.

Gradually, as my father's business succeeded, my mother began to see herself as the "lady of the manor" and patronized her less fortunate sisters. My father indulged her and she was able to buy the beautiful clothes she had been denied. She had, in fact, everything she wanted, except respect and love.

She died at the age of 102, never having had a day's illness, but her life was an empty shell. She never did anything creative or went anywhere interesting, neither to the theatre or a concert, a library or a museum, was not interested in the arts, never listened to music, never read a book except cheap romantic novels, saw no value in education. I feel so very sorry that this woman, my mother, had so many chances to enrich her life and ours, but was only interested in herself.

Brown Egg

Warm brown egg
fresh from the hen
lies in my hand,
Sweet, warm
smell of the byre.
Dipper to scoop
and fling the grain
to the waiting hens.

Lift the lid
of the nesting box
and find another
warm brown egg.

The Story of My Education or Lack of It!

I have written extensively about my education, or to be truthful, the lack of it! I ran away to school at the age of four, my fourth birthday, to be precise, because more than anything I wanted to go to school, I wanted to learn.

My father had taught me to write my name, I knew my ABCs, and I could spell OXO, BOVRIL, and PEARS SOAP, from the big billboards outside on the street, and I could count.

There was no television and very little radio in those days, only very rudimentary scratchy voices came and went, accompanied by loud whistles and squeaks, through a large horn in our house.

But I loved the stories my father read to me, and I wanted to be able to read them myself. This was the reason I packed a little notebook and pencil into a small bag, crept quietly down the iron staircase to the garden, through the wooden gate and up the road towards the school.

Harry lived next door and went to school. Harry was six, and so I figured I could go too, I was nearly six after all. I joined the children playing in the schoolyard, and when the teacher came out with the big bell, I simply followed them inside.

Sadly I was discovered, but spent a blissful morning in the classroom until it was time to go home. I don't know how my parents explained to me why I would not be able to go back the next day.

I was six before I was old enough to start school in earnest, and by then, 1932, we had moved to another district. Thus I was not able to go to the charming little school I ran away to. We lived on the boundary of a very poor working-class area, and there was only one school I could attend, and it was a terrible school, gloomy and old with large overcrowded classes. Some of the children wore ragged clothes, others had leg irons, caused I learned later, by rickets, or malnutrition. They were unruly, rough and coarse. The teacher had a tough time controlling a class of 52 noisy children, but she did, with the use of a cane!

From day one, my education failed me. What I did learn was that to be accepted, it was not smart to be clever. I remember how shocked I was in those days. I had been so eager to learn.

I was abused by the teacher for refusing to go into the hall for morning prayers. She physically shook me, and forced me, screaming and crying, to join the rest of the students. The reason for my fear of religion is another story, of being taken at age five to my grandmother's Chapel, an austere and fearsome place which terrified me, and has left its mark to this day.

The children at that school ganged up on this shy little girl, and I very quickly learned that in order to fit in I had to forget my desire to learn and be smart. It died within me.

I don't remember any teacher taking me aside and saying "You can do better than

31

this". I don't remember my parents saying it either, nobody seemed to care, so I gave up trying, almost relishing my sliding grades. There was no incentive to do well.

When World War II began, all schools in cities were closed, the students were evacuated to safer country towns and we lived in foster homes.

Schools were shared between their students and ours; they attended in the mornings and we went in the afternoons. There was a lot of homework and left alone to work I fell behind.

I can't blame the school I attended, or the war, I had lost my desire to succeed, and I think the lack of encouragement was to blame.

When the blitz became more intensive, my father sent me to his hometown in the North of Scotland to live with my grandmother. My younger sister, Doris, was already there, and I was registered at the local Academy, the same school my father had attended as a boy.

This school was different. Much was expected, and to my consternation, the principal took me aside one day, and explained gently that my grades were not good enough for the class of children my own age, and that it would be better for me to be transferred to a lower class. I was so humiliated when I had to explain to my family what had happened that day. It was a jolt, though, one that I needed and I knew what I had to do. All my aunts and uncles as well as my father had been to Forres Academy, I had a great reputation to uphold, and I couldn't let them down.

I also had at least three teachers, called back from retirement, who had taught my father. So I worked hard that year, was happier than I had ever been before, and I did well.

Sadly, my mother who did not get along with her Scottish in-laws, decided to go back to London, and of course, Doris and I had to go too. So once again our education was interrupted, and I returned to Latymer (my original school) which had re-opened with a skeleton staff, and students like myself, all at different levels, none of us knowing where we stood. The valuable work ethics I learned at Forres Academy deteriorated. I begged my father to let me leave school, and he did. Looking back I wonder why? A Scotsman, coming from a country where education is so important, and from a school where I did so well. Why didn't he send me back? I have a sneaking suspicion he didn't want to pay the fees for Latymer. That's a terrible thought I know, but I remember him saying once, "You're just a dunderhead (dummy) I'm not wasting money on your education. You'll never make anything of yourself, you'll just get married anyway".

I regret very much not being able to finish my education, I was just fourteen years old when I left school, much too young to make decisions that would determine my future.

I went to work helping my father in his shop. He was a pharmacist and had a thriving business, he needed the help and to be truthful I enjoyed those three years working there. I liked people, and I know the customers liked me; I was good at my job. The hours were long, nine hours a day, six days a week with a halfday on Thursdays, but twelve hours on

Saturdays. I had to bicycle seven miles to work and back, often with air raids overhead, and in all weather, because I didn't earn enough for the bus fare.

Doris had a similar experience, although when she left school at fifteen, my father sent her to a Business School. She also worked in the shop for very little money. There was no future for either of us, except marriage, which in those days, was the expected life for girls. College was an unknown word in Britain.

My education flourished when I joined the British Women's Army in the Auxiliary Territorial Service (the A.T.S.) at age eighteen, and became an army driver for three years at the end of World War II and beyond. I gained self-esteem and was able to accept responsibility. I loved my army experience, and was comfortable with my peers, and with the officers I sometimes drove. I never saluted, opened car doors or called them "Sir" or "Ma'am". One of them kissed me once through the open window, a dark-haired, blue-eyed Irishman with a sassy brogue and a naughty twinkle in his eyes!

It's likely I would not have been in the military if I'd gone back to Forres Academy. I wouldn't have met Anthony, my husband of sixty years, and had the fascinating life I have had.

So maybe fate does have a hand in the way things materialize, although nothing just happens on it's own, you have to "stir the pot" I believe, and certainly my pot has had a great deal of stirring. And in spite of everything, I finished up with a very rich soup!

Aunt Phil

Aunt Phil was my mother's younger sister. She was without doubt, the wild one in the family. "She'll come to no good" my mother would say ominously. But I have heard that Aunt Phil laughed and danced her way through her teenage years, not caring what anyone said or thought, and I imagine, having a high old time.

She apparently fluffed her hair into a fuzzy mop in the fashion of the day, flashing her dark eyes, and flirting outrageously with every man in sight.

It was said that she wrote to the film studios, enclosing a photograph of herself in a 1920's style short dress with long beads wearing a sultry expression on her face, and a long cigarette holder held delicately in her fingers, offering to come for a screen test. I'm not sure she ever received a reply, and sadly I don't have that photo.

Well of course the inevitable happened, and at 16 she "had to get married" as they said in those days.

After her children were born, four of them, I know from here on that Aunt Phil went out to work. She cleaned houses, she helped out in the fields when it was harvest time and continued to laugh at life. "She looks like a gypsy" said my mother "common as dirt. We don't want her kind around here."

But my sister, Doris and I liked Aunt Phil when she came to visit. She played skipping games with us, and hop scotch, and got down on the ground to play marbles.

And much later on, during the war she arrived with a large empty suitcase, and filled it with my mother's left-off clothes in exchange for black market clothing coupons – a precious commodity in those days of shortages.

When we moved to Scotland, Aunt Phil still came to visit, and my mother continued to pour scorn on her less-than-desirable behaviour.

Ironically though, when my mother broke her hip and needed help, it was Aunt Phil who made the long overnight journey by train and came to the rescue, to clean and shop and cook and help my mother get on her feet again.

Only then did mother realize that her sister was worth her weight in gold and regretted the years of wasted fun and laughter she could have had, that Aunt Phil always brought with her.

Nanny

When my grandmother came to visit it was a dreaded occasion. She slept in my room and prayed a lot. "Have mercy" she would say over and over again "Have mercy Lord". I wasn't quite sure what mercy meant, except that there was a girl in my class named Mercy Woodhouse, but somehow I didn't think it had anything to do with her, I hoped not.

Doris and I called our grandmother "Nanny". She was tall and thin with black hair screwed tightly into a bun, a brown face like a withered old apple, and her mouth was a tight straight line, and she arrived bearing a big black cloud, and some religious books for us, with gruesome pictures. We didn't look forward to Nanny's visits, she made us feel as though we had a lot of nice things that other poor little girls didn't have. It made us feel guilty that we had so many luxuries, which we didn't have as far as I could see, and we should give everything to Nanny to take to the poor little girls she knew, who didn't have anything.

We had to say grace when Nanny came, bow our heads and thank the Lord for what we were about to receive. Personally I didn't think he was anywhere around when my mother cooked supper, otherwise we would have had more puddings and cake and ice cream instead of all the slimy cabbage and greens we had to eat.

Sometimes Nanny went into the bathroom to pray, and since it was the only bathroom we had, we had to wait outside, which was not always very convenient.

And at night when we went to bed she would fall on her knees beside the bed to pray in her white nightgown with her long black hair around her shoulders. Her prayers started softly, but got louder and louder as time went on. Mixed up were a lot of "mercys".

I hid under the blankets just in case she called God into the room. I didn't want him to know I was such a selfish little girl with all those good things I didn't deserve.

The sun seemed to shine brighter when Nanny went home and took her black cloud with her.

Later though, much later on, Nanny became quite a gal. She left her religion behind and came by herself. She wore dresses with colour and quite stylish hats, and shoes with little heels. She came with a twinkle in her eye and a smile, and books in her bag to read on the train that were the slightest bit naughty.

Yes, we liked Nanny a lot more after that.

Revelation - First Light

It was the summer of my "Growing Up" years; I was about 15 years old. The spring had been a season of smothering of ideas that blossomed in my young mind. So I had turned inward, caring deeply what other people might think of me, a copy of my mother.

But despite the tight rein put on me, my ideas overflowed. I wrote plays for the neighborhood kids to perform, and perform them we did, on the patio of our backyard.

I wrote poetry, and painted wild undisciplined paintings, way outside the lines. Colors that blended with other colors, creating magical shapes.

I made theaters out of cardboard boxes, with curtains and sets, and paper puppets that danced on strings.

There were lectures of disapproval from my parents. "A waste of time" they said. "Do your schoolwork, concentrate on math and science" they said. "Art School was out of the question" they said.

The rebel in me took root.

Then one day, all alone in my room "to think about things," a revelation swept over me.

I was myself, I am myself. I am a special person with thoughts and loves and talents all my own. Nobody else's, just mine, and nobody can take them away from me.

Suddenly, I didn't care what other people thought of me. I would become what I set out to be. I would create beautiful things in my own way, and I would not be molded into somebody I was not.

At that moment, a huge load fell away from me, and I looked in the mirror and saw myself for the very first time.

The Sands of Findhorn

Findhorn is a tiny town on the Moray Firth just before it widens into the North Sea.

Little one-story granite houses dot the Bay, nothing much else. A corner grocery store where you can buy bread and cheese, apples and canned food, served by an elderly smiling couple. An ice cream shop where you can also buy fizzy lemonade in bottles, and postcards of local views, pictures of men in kilts playing bagpipes, and Scottish terriers and West Highland terriers sitting side-by-side, and sprigs of white heather.

A winding cobbled street threads them altogether like beads. One hotel standing alone at the edge of the dunes on the Back Shore. Mostly though, the little blue country bus brings in day trippers from Forres five miles away.

My grandmother and two unmarried aunts lived in Forres, and as children and teenagers, my sister and I rode our bicycles to Findhorn with our bathing suits, towels, and a packed lunch in baskets on the handlebars.

The beach at Findhorn, smelling of seaweed and clean salt air, stretched from the Bay, mile after golden mile along the coast to the fishing village of Burghead. Bordering the beach were sand dunes that provided warm sandy depressions laced with sea grass where we could eat our lunch sheltered from the wind, and change into bathing suits, leave our clothes and bicycles and run across the flat hard sand to the sea.

Oh that beach! You can find shells and translucent stones, which could be cut into cairngorms if you were lucky enough to be able to see the sun through them, but we never were. And pieces of green glass pounded into smooth shapes by ancient seas, and left by the tides in the warm shallow pools, perfect for us as young children to wade and play.

We loved Findhorn. I remember the happy sunlit days we spent there so long ago, it is still more or less the same after all these years, isolated, and undisturbed by crowds of noisy tourists, just visited and revisited by the grown-up children like my sister and me.

Findhorn Bay

Mouse

Down - soft, cloud - soft,

Large eyes searching.

Knowing but unknowing ever searching

ever searching.

Shadow drifting.

Scamper - quick, now burrow quickly.

Dig down, cover, cover quickly.

Sweet grass keep me hidden

From the fearsome shadow

drifting, drifting.

Rocks Exposed

Hidden under the roots

of the old tree

it came to life at last

in the sun.

Colored long ago

when the earth

was molten.

Invaded by

Stripes of quartz,

and spirits

who live in rocks,

now free to dance

in the sun.

Winter Wind

Wind

    Shrieking in from the west

    or the north

    or both,

Shrieking, screaming

    from the mountains

    down across

    the valleys.

Whistling, swirling

    through the terrified

    branches

breaking them,

    tossing them

    through the air.

Skimming snow

    across the frozen lakes

    shifting waves

    of snow.

Penetrating

    all I have on

    pushing the breath

back down

    into my body

Turn around, turn around,

    wind lifts me

    tosses me

back to the blessed shelter

    of my car.

Evacuation Train

September 3rd, 1939 was the day Britain declared war on Germany.

I was thirteen with a mind of my own and a desire to know everything that was going on in the world, and be part of it. I lived in a very restrictive household and until my teenage years, my mother didn't "spare the rod". I couldn't wait to leave home and be myself, and the war years were to determine my future, and made me who I am today.

That summer though, 1939, Britain had to prepare for the war we knew was coming. Hitler had marched his troops into the Sudetenland in Czechoslovakia, then Austria and the low countries Belgium, Holland, and Denmark, and then he turned his attention to Poland.

Britain sent an ultimatum, if he marched into Poland, Britain would go to war! The Prime Minister, Neville Chamberlain flew to Germany and met with Hitler. They signed a non-aggression pact, but it meant nothing. Mr. Chamberlain returned to Britain and waved his piece of paper, "Peace in our Time" he said. That same week Hitler bombed Warsaw, and Britain was at war with Germany. World War II had begun.

Throughout the summer though, preparations were made. Sirens were installed and tested, long wailing notes, and the "All Clear", a long continual sound. Air Raid shelters were delivered, one to each family. These were u-shaped pieces of corrugated iron, 3' for each family member, so as a family of four we were allotted four sections and our shelter measured 12' x 8'.

My father dug a hole in the backyard, it needed to be 4' deep, and with a neighbor's help, maneuvered those heavy pieces of metal into place, and then they were bolted together from the inside.

My sister Doris and I chinked all the cracks with wet newspaper, and then we helped shovel dirt back on top and packed it down. My Dad cemented the floor, and built a brick wall around the outside for extra reinforcement. It was really quite exciting for us kids and I remember wanting to sleep in it right away. We had to be fitted for gas masks, nasty rubbery things with an eyepiece and a round filter on the front.

Young men who were eligible for service were put on reserve, and trained in the use of World War I rifles. The older men were given training as Air Raid Wardens. They wore steel helmets with a big white "W" on the front, and were taught how to extinguish incendiary bombs, using a stirrup pump and bucket of water, and a trash can lid as a shield.

How essential all this training was later on when incendiary bombs rained down upon our cities.

Detailed evacuation plans were put into place for the transportation of children out of the cities to the safety of the countryside, and rehearsals were held at all schools. It was decided that I would go with my school, while Doris would go to our grandmother's in the North of Scotland accompanied by my aunt with her newborn baby.

Women had to buy blackout material and made curtains for every window, because not a chink of light must show, and windows were to have strips of sticky brown tape criss-crossed over the glass to prevent shattering in the event of a bomb blast. But then of course, towards the end of summer, it ceased to be fun, as we all realized how serious it all was.

Ration books were issued for every family member and luxury items began to disappear from store shelves. We in Britain were so dependent on food coming across the Atlantic, and oranges, lemons, and bananas were the first to go. Canned fruit, meat, and fish, like salmon, butter, eggs and cheese from Holland and France, tea and coffee were in short supply, everything that was imported in fact.

September 2nd, we children had to report to our schools in the morning with one small suitcase, our gas masks in a box with a string to go over our shoulders, and to be wearing our winter uniforms: tunics and blouses, sweaters, and coats and hats, long black stockings and black lace-up shoes, and September was very warm that year.

My father drove me to school, I don't remember saying good-bye, so excited was I. We all assembled on the school playing-field, long lines of children, and we sang "Roll Out The Barrel" and "South of the Border Down Mexico Way". And then it was time to go. There were no buses to carry all of us, and so we walked in twos to the railway station. It was a long way for little siblings, so the bigger students and teachers carried them on their backs. There we were, name tags fluttering from our buttonholes, passing through lines of moms watching us go, some were crying, but they all waved as we went by, and shouted encouragement. It was the same in all the cities all over the country, long lines of children converging on railway stations and the waiting trains.

Our train stood waiting, big signs in all the windows "Evacuation Train". Everybody boarded, and with a whistle from the engine, a lurch, and loud puffing, the train pulled out of the station. Nobody knew where we were going, except the teachers of course. All rail traffic was put on hold, as the evacuation trains sped non-stop to their destinations, it was a tremendous piece of organization.

So it was such a surprise then, when we arrived at a small seaside resort on the East Coast of England, about as close as you could get to the German air fields across the North Sea. Whose bright idea was that I wonder?

In retrospect, how hard it must have been for parents to let their children go, to be cared for by people they didn't know, maybe with different ideas about raising children and with different values, and some not used to children at all. For me it was a great adventure, I was never very close to my parents, and relished the idea of getting away.

On arrival at Clacton-on-Sea, we were again marched to a school outside the town where we were given sandwiches and juice, then divided into groups of about 25. Our group went to a district of small modest homes escorted by a teacher and a billeting officer from the town. We stood in the middle of the road, rather forlorn and anxious as the two men went house to house, and each student was allotted a foster home.

When it was my turn, the woman who opened the door said she could take three students. Our teacher then went in to inspect the accommodation and found she wanted to put three of us into one bed! Two of us finished up going to live with Mrs. Clark. She was a dour pale-faced woman with sparse sandy hair and had no children of her own. To have two teenagers suddenly dumped on her must have been daunting. Suddenly the great adventure became rather frightening, here we were in a strange town, living with a woman who obviously wasn't very happy to see us, but foster parents would be getting extra rations, and an allowance from the government, perhaps this was the reasoning to take in evacuees.

That evening we had a meal of cold canned corned beef and boiled potatoes, and attempted some strained conversation, then we went outside to meet our classmates and discuss our different situations. None of us happy with our changed lifestyles, but we realized even at that tender age that we'd better make the best of it.

As it turned out, my roommate's parents came to visit, summed up the situation and moved us to a Miss Wrampling, who ran a small hotel, had plenty of rooms, and moreover was very anxious to have us. In the end there were eight of us living with Miss Wrampling, a welcome change, from Mrs. Clark.

We shared the local high school with the students already there, they went in the mornings and we in the afternoons, and had lots of homework.

The first three months of World War II were called the "phoney war", we expected air raids and nothing happened. One lone German plane crashed close by, and a lot of the townspeople went to the funeral of the pilot, and took flowers. "Some mother's son" was the sympathetic comment we heard.

The long wet autumn dragged on and after Christmas 1939, many parents wanted their children back since it seemed safe, and so a lot of us went home.

Back in London we found there were no schools, all had been closed because of the evacuation, but my Dad found a small private school, and I went there for a short time feeling like a fish out of water, but at least I was able to continue my education.

And then the London blitz began!

Memories of an Ordinary British Woman

The sirens went at 9 p.m. They always went at 9 p.m. just as the evening news was beginning. Far away we could hear sirens in other towns, gradually getting closer until our local one sounded, a warning to us all to get to a safe place.

There were three of us, my mother, father and I, living in an apartment over my father's pharmacy on the northern edge of London, I was fourteen years old. Outside we could see over a good part of the city, and as we hurried down the staircase leading to the backyard, and our little air raid shelter, we saw the flashes, heard the distant rumble of gunfire, and could see the great sweeping arcs of searchlights as they probed the sky for enemy planes. We carried with us blankets, pillows and hot water bottles, a basket of sandwiches and a thermos of hot tea, knowing that this was going to be another night in our little hole in the ground.

Once inside the shelter, which measured about 8' x 12', we groped for matches and lit candles. It was dark and damp and smelled of mildew and candle smoke. My father had found a couple of old car seats. He had cemented the floor and put down a piece of matting, and we had two wooden orange crates to store our first-aid kits, some plates and cups, and a supply of candles. At the back of the shelter was an emergency exit and a shovel, in case a bomb dropped close by and we weren't able to use the front door. So we were as prepared as we could possibly be, but it wasn't exactly "home from home".

Sometimes the raid took place over South London and the middle of the city, but often we could hear the sound of planes approaching from a different direction, and then our own guns just down the road, would open up and the noise was deafening as they poured shells into the dark sky. There was no peering out to see what was going on at this point, because jagged pieces of shrapnel came raining down. My father, who was an air raid Warden, would have to patrol when there was a lull to make sure there were no fires from incendiary bombs, and if so, all the neighboring men would put them out with stirrup pumps if possible.

We began to recognize the sound of the planes' engines, the throbbing note of the German planes, "one of theirs" we'd say knowingly, and it was borne out when a bomb came whistling down. I swear they put whistles on their bombs to scare us, but I don't know for sure, it just sounded like it.

Sometimes though, sticks of bombs dropped uncomfortably close, the walls of our little shelter shuddered, and grit fell on us through the cracks in the ceiling. The flames from the candles shook and wavered when this happened, but continued to burn, cheering us in those dark moments. "That was a close one" Dad would say, and when a lull came he went outside to see if there was any damage to the house. "Just a few windows broken, that's all" he said when he returned. The lull was also an opportunity for me to say I absolutely had to go to the bathroom, which of course was in the house, and then I was also able to have a good look at the raid going on over London. But it was dangerous, and it wasn't long before my Dad came looking for me.

My 9-year-old sister had been evacuated to Northern Scotland where our grandmother lived, and looking at my mother sitting pale and trembling, it was clear she should have gone too.

The raids seemed to be concentrated mainly on the London docks just to the south of us, where 'pathfinders' flew up the Thames to drop incendiary bombs on the areas bordering the river, the heavy bombers came after them following the fires that were started. These fires consumed the small homes there, the East End, where the true Londoners lived, the Cockneys, proud strong people who suffered more than anybody during the blitz, but never lost their sense of humor.

They were driven to the subways (the tube) deep down underground where they were safe. In the beginning they slept side-by-side along the platforms while train passengers had to step carefully over them. Later on, bunks were built against the walls, and every evening there would be a party going on, or a sing-song. In the mornings they would all emerge like moles often to damaged or destroyed homes or little shops, where they would sweep away the broken glass, and put up signs that read "_____ you Hitler. Business as usual!" And the women would go back to work cleaning offices, with smiles on their faces. These were wonderful, wonderful people, so proud to be Londoners.

It was at times like these that Winston Churchill gave one of his magnificent speeches. We listened spellbound, and afterwards stood a little taller. Never, ever, did we think we would be beaten. All of us stood together, all involved in some way or other, "The Auxiliary Fire Service", "The Women's Voluntary Service" who ran canteens, the Home Guard, often ex-servicemen from World War I, glad to be called upon to help defend their country, if the need came.

Even teenagers like myself joined pre-service training units where we learned first-aid, and CPR, morse code and how to use radios. We all stood resolutely behind Winston Churchill, our Prime Minister, who had formed a coalition government, which worked amazingly well. We had different departments like the Ministry of Food, the Ministry of Health, the Ministry of Agriculture and Fisheries, Ministry of Energy and Ministry of Transport, and so on, all working side by side for the good of the country. Politics were set aside.

With very little food we learned to cook differently. Flyers were sent out telling us how to make meals out of what we had – nothing was wasted – and how to cook vegetables to conserve vitamins. Children collected rosehips when they were in season, and took them to collection stations where they were made into a syrup, and wonderful it was too for sweetening fruit.

Across the Atlantic came dried eggs, dried milk, mashed potato powder, and Spam. How we devoured that Spam! And believe it or not I still like Spam. People of my generation will never forget the food that was sent from America at the risk of many lives, that literally saved us from starvation.

Then came the summer of 1940 when Churchill announced in one of his speeches "The Battle of France is over, the Battle of Britain is about to begin", and so it did. Germany began heavy daylight raids as well as at night, but this time they had to contend with the Hurricanes and Spitfires, and the very young men who flew them.

Waves of German bombers flew in large formations across the English Channel from France. Time and time again these amazing young men went up to tackle them. We watched battle after battle from below, all of us cheering when a Spitfire did a victory roll. Many were lost and pilots too, and all the while the aircraft factories worked 24-7 producing more planes, and the flying schools trained more young pilots, some as young as 18. But at the end of the summer Hitler gave up and the Battle of Britain was won.

Then Churchill said, "Never in the field of human conflict has so much been owed by so many, to so few."

As I write this now, I feel so emotional and so proud to have been a part of all that. It was a terrible war for so many people, but for us in Britain it brought out the very best in all of us. There had been some very dark times but we knew it was far from over, there would be a lot of hardships ahead of us.

I think if Germany had won the Battle of Britain, we would have been invaded, and it was certain to have been all over, but not without a fight from all of us ordinary folk, you can be sure of that.

The Way It Was

One cold night in early spring of 1940, my mother and I were making our way to one of London's main railway stations to travel to the north of Scotland.

It had been a brutal few months of bombing, and the blitz showed no sign of coming to an end. We had spent every night in a little bomb shelter in our backyard, a space roughly 12' x 8' dug down 4' into the ground, dark, except for a couple of candles, a blanket covering the doorway, two old car seats my father had found somewhere, and a piece of matting on the floor. It was cold and damp and musty, there wasn't room to lie down, so we sat all night trying to sleep which was difficult anyway, with the noise of the big guns just down the road and the constant sound of aircraft overhead.

The raids had become worse of late, and my father insisted we go north to his family in Scotland. My mother needed a rest, she was a nervous woman at the best of times, and so I was given the tickets and instructions and charge of my mother, a lot of responsibility for a 14-year-old. But I felt confident. I had traveled many times on this train, I knew the way to go. We grew up fast in those days.

The 7:10 train to Inverness was standing at the station - no trains were leaving while the raid was on, so we boarded and found our seats by flashlights. No lights were allowed, all the windows blacked out. We found the train packed with soldiers rescued from the beaches of Dunkirk (another story). They were filthy dirty, mud-caked and exhausted, lying on the floors, in the corridors, even in the toilets. Their eyes filled with the despair of failure.

We sat waiting for the raid to end, no one spoke. Around us the cacophony of gunfire, the heavy drone of many aircraft and the whistle and explosions of bombs.

We all knew the railway stations were prime targets, yet we sat motionless as if by moving or speaking the bombs would be directed to us.

The lull came, finally, and the train drifted slowly out of the station, picking up speed until slowed by yet another raid over yet another town, waiting again in silence.

It seemed like hours before the train moved faster and continued north through the night. As dawn approached, and after many stops and starts, I went into the corridor and opened a window and saw the gentle hills of the border country, as we climbed into the craggy highlands of Scotland.

Streams rushed downhill, sheep grazed, the small country station gardens tended by the station masters were filled with daffodils. Behind me those desperately tired soldiers straight from the beaches of France, slept in peace in another world.

The Beginning of the End

I was in London when the Americans came to Britain, and it was as though they had invaded our country, undoubtedly they took over London that day I first set eyes upon them.

They were certainly different, in the way they walked, they had an easy rolling gait, a kind of swagger. They were very self-assured, or so it seemed to us, their uniforms were smart and well cut, they chewed gum, they bragged, and we weren't quite sure about that, because Brits don't brag, but they were far from home so we forgave them.

All the girls were bowled over by those fresh-faced, smiling young men with their friendly ways and good manners, but it caused some trouble with our boys in their rough unattractive uniforms who had nothing much to smile about. Stealing our girls could not be tolerated, and there were often fights in pubs and on the streets.

American soldiers also seemed to have a lot of money to spend, and a generous supply of cigarettes, candy, and nylon stockings. Oh those nylon stockings!

We called them "Yanks" because to be truthful, we didn't know much about the American Civil War, and the differences that remain to this day between the North and South. It would be like calling a Scotsman an Englishman. Not done!

But that day in London, those lovely young men turned the city upside down. They held up traffic in Picadilly, they rode on the roofs of our staid London taxis, and hung onto the sides, singing and whistling at the girls. They climbed onto the big bronze lions in Trafalgar Square, and everybody loved them. Even our rather sombre British bobbies smiled and didn't try to stop the high jinx. Soon enough those young soldiers would face the horrors of war.

The next two years brought many changes. My father sent me to the School of Photography at the Regent Street Polytechnic in the center of London, and I supposed it was the next best thing to Art School which is where I really wanted to go, but it was there after all that I met my future husband Anthony Barringer who was studying math and physics in the same building.

Because the air raids were so intense, my mother and sister were once again sent to Scotland, but this time I stayed behind in London with my father and continued my training as a photographer. Life was very uncertain in those days, we didn't think much about our future, we didn't know whether there would even be one.

However, it wasn't all doom and gloom. There were dances every Saturday night, and I was allowed to go providing I went with a group of girls and came back with them. I should mention that I was seventeen, but life and rules were very different then. Most of the young men had been called up. There were plenty of boys our age, but still a surplus of girls, and since none of us had partners, we danced with each other.

The dance hall was always crowded, and there was a giant silver ball made up of mirrors, that hung in the middle which rotated, sending sparkly lights round the room. A band played Big Band music, and we swung and jitterbugged, eyeing the boys and hoping to be asked to dance, which didn't happen very often, but we all had a very good time, then headed out into the blacked-out streets to walk home.

We went about our days and nights as though there were no air raids going on around us, diving into a public air raid shelter if things got a bit too close for comfort, but the raids became a part of our lives, and we just ignored them.

Everybody listened avidly to the news as the action spread from North Africa to Crete and Italy, from good news to bad and back again. We wondered at the time when D-Day would happen, knowing that intensive training was going on. Knowing also that now our own air forces were flying into enemy territories. The RAF in Lancaster bombers at night, and the American B17s or Flying Fortresses by day.

For the longest time when Britain was fighting alone, we weren't able to do this, and had to defend our own country, depending mainly on fighter planes such as Spitfires and Hurricanes. But with the addition of the American Army Air Corps, as it was then, we were able to turn things around and go on the offensive.

The Germans were sending V1's (flying bombs) launched from Northern France and dropping mainly on South London, "Doodlebug Alley" we called it, some being shot down, but many getting through. This was indiscriminate bombing, not being aimed at targets, but on the ordinary people of London.

I can remember Anthony and I sitting on the Thames Embankment as hundreds of planes towing gliders flew past heading south, and we knew it was D-Day, June 6th, 1944. We looked at each other, knowing how much depended on those men in the gliders flying towards France.

At every news broadcast, we stopped whatever we were doing to listen, and I can well remember the announcer in his correct BBC English saying "We interrupt this program to bring you a bulletin", and then would come a piece of news related directly from the invasion by the crackly voice of Walter Kronkite or Ed Murrow. They certainly were exciting times.

Both Anthony and I were approaching eighteen, and young people our age were being called up for military service, and so it was that both of us were called up about the same time. Anthony trained for the Parachute Regiment, while I went to the Army Driver Training School. Women did not go into combat in World War II, but were enlisted to replace the men who did, and all men were required at that time for armed combat. Young women who were not in what they called "reserved occupations" were drafted into the services.

In 1945 the war in Europe ended and Anthony and I stood in the rain in Picadilly when the lights came on after six years of darkness. We cheered ourselves hoarse on VE Day, standing on a wall and watching the victory parade march along the Mall, we danced in the streets, and yelled for the King outside Buckingham Palace along with thousands of other happy people.

Otherwise though, life was still tough. There weren't any jobs for returning servicemen, food was still rationed, young couples had to live with in-laws. But Australia and Canada came to the rescue and encouraged young people to emigrate, offering cheap fares by sea, and jobs, and many people did that, including ourselves in 1954. The war was over and that's all that mattered, we could put up with a few more hardships.

I am very proud to have been born British and lived there through those dark days in our broken war-torn country. We blessed Canada and Australia for opening their arms to us in welcome, and we blessed America for literally saving us from starvation, and sending their young men to our aid when we most needed it, helping to liberate the whole of Europe from Nazi domination.

Saving the Harvest

It was the summer of 1942, the middle of the war, and with all the young men gone, the farmers were desperate for help in the fields.

Posters appeared in bus and train stations and in the newspapers asking people to spend their vacations at farming camps all over the country.

"Help your country bring in the harvest" they said, "Spend a healthy two weeks in the country – food and lodging provided."

So we went, my friend Maureen and I, and Maureen's cousins and parents, along with hundreds of others, by special train to a town a hundred or so miles north of London where we were met by buses and transported to various farming camps in the area.

The camp was set up in a field, large family-size tents with cots, and an extra large mess tent and cook house, army style.

We had been told to bring sheets, and working clothes, overalls and sturdy shoes, in the days when it was rare for women to wear trousers. I had bought a pair of bib overalls, I didn't have enough clothing coupons to buy 2 pairs.

We were issued blankets, tin plates and mugs, knives, forks and spoons, and settled in, work would begin next morning. Everybody met for supper in the mess tent at long tables and benches, and met other campers who had been there longer, tired and sunburned from a day in the fields mostly students, and some German Jewish refugees, learning some English and earning a little bit of money.

Next morning after a breakfast of scrambled eggs and toast, we were required to peel three potatoes before lining up for work. The farmers arrived with their trucks to pick up their workers, a dozen here, a dozen there, we scrambled aboard the trucks amid much laughter as the older people amongst us had to be helped up with undignified difficulty.

Every day something different. We lifted potatoes, back-breaking work all day; we cut greens off turnips with lethal looking scythes, stacked wheat into sheaves, cut away brush from hillsides, clearing land for planting next season. We cut seed-heads off onion plants and put them in sacks.

There were Italian prisoners-of-war helping, singing as they worked, glad to be out of the war. They called me Gina!

Lunch was brought to us wherever we were, crusty bread from the bakery, strong yellow cheese, and fresh milk from a dairy farm. It was a feast.

We did everything we were asked to do, a motley crowd of ordinary people, young and middle-aged who had never worked so hard before. And at the end of each day we were again loaded into the backs of trucks weary and hungry, and each of us was given a small amount of pay.

And so, all over Britain, camps such as ours had been set up, and the harvest was brought in by hundreds of ordinary people just like us!

The Folly of Youth

Anthony and I sat in the bus as it jounced its way across the bridge to London's South Bank. It was the spring of 1944, and Tony and I had skipped classes to go on this crazy adventure.

It was an old rather battered bus, filled with Londoners going who knows where, many of them having been bombed out perhaps more than once. But Londoners are a tough breed, and adversity made them all the more determined to stick together.

Now after five years of constant bombing they were very tired, undernourished, and decidedly down-at-heel, but discouraged – never!

South London was Doodlebug Alley, and Doodlebugs, to those uninitiated souls, was the Londener's name for V1's, the pilot-less aircraft fired by the Germans towards London in the latter part of World War II.

A lot were shot down by fighter pilots before they reached London, but many, many more got through. Forced through the air by a jet engine, a bright flame spewing from its tail the engine would suddenly cut out, and the Doodlebug would then dive towards the ground, demolishing all in its path.

There were no military targets – this was indiscriminate bombing of homes belonging to the little people who refused to leave London at the height of the war.

For young folk at that time, life was one huge adventure. We didn't think of the future, there may not be one, life was "now".

We gave not a single thought to our parents, so completely unaware of our escapade, but at seventeen you didn't tell your parents such things.

The bus moved slowly along the sunlit street, bombed houses on one side, a green leafy park on the other. The air-raid sirens sounded, the bus drove on as if nothing had happened; the air-raid sirens' up-and-down wails were so commonplace that nobody took any notice anymore and simply carried on with whatever they were doing.

Suddenly above the noise of the bus engine came that high-pitched piercing whine that was unmistakable. The driver wasted no time and pulled over to the side of the road. "Everyone off" he shouted, and we did just that, not to the shelter close by however.

Tony grabbed my hand and we swung across the road and into the park. Looking up, immediately above us we could see the Doodlebug, the sound of its engine deafening now it was so close.

Suddenly the noise stopped, but it was as if it still hung in the air, as if everyone held their breath.

Tony and I flung ourselves down as the plane hit the ground about 500 yards away with a tremendous explosion hurling debris in all directions.

The earth shook, and so did I–it was something I wouldn't forget, and haven't after all these years. We were lucky to have survived that adventure–and I never did tell my parents.

The Turning Point

As the war progressed, girls as well as boys were called up when they reached the age of eighteen, and so I, along with thousands of other young people received our call-up papers at that time.

The men were all overseas of course, and the Services needed girls to fill in where we were needed most. I had enlisted before I reached eighteen so that I would have more choice, but there was no guarantee as to where we would be placed, or what we would be required to do.

So one morning early in January 1945, I went to Victoria Station in the center of London and joined a group of thirty other young women waiting to be escorted to Training Camp at Guildford in Surrey, south of London. The Officer in charge was able to answer the hundred and one questions we asked, but nothing really prepared us for what was to follow.

The Training Camp for the Auxiliary Territorial Service (ATS) was a large area filled with about fifty barrack-huts for twenty four recruits each, iron cots, a potbelly stove in the middle, and a washroom, called ablutions, at each end.

There was a parade ground, a mess-hall, and quartermaster store. There was a CRS, (a hospital) and medical center, a lecture hall, and a guard post at the gate, so that nobody could slip out! We were to be there for three weeks and the discipline was fierce.

We were issued with khaki uniforms that first day, scratchy and not very well fitting. My skirt was too long and I shortened it, only to be hauled up in front of quartermaster, a sour-faced sergeant, to "Let it down. Immediately." I was not allowed to argue, or say anything, my skirt had to stay the way it was, long!

We were vaccinated against small-pox and inoculated against tetanus, typhoid and diphtheria, and even though our arms swelled and hurt abominably, we were required to assemble on the drill square and march with our arms swinging shoulder-high, British fashion. There were no excuses, even though some of us were running a low fever. Rules were rules.

We learned to strip our beds every morning and fold the blankets and sheets, with one blanket folded like a package around all of them. We had to lay our kit out on the bed in correct order, and then we, in full uniform with hats on straight, stood at attention while the officer with the hut sergeant, inspected the kit and ourselves head to toe, back and front. Hair had to be off the collar, buttons polished, and shoes as shiny as we could possibly make them. I'll tell you, spit and polish is absolutely true where shoes are concerned.

Food in the mess was inedible, greasy and disgusting. But we weren't allowed to leave any of it. A sergeant stood at the door to make sure nothing was thrown away. We washed our plates and mugs in a tub of hot water which was pretty dirty after everyone had used it!

Drill was every day, so were long-distance route marches, and phys ed. There were lectures on military law and tests to be taken. Our hats had to be worn at all times when we were outside, we learned to call officers Ma'am and salute when we encountered one. They were three grueling weeks, reveille was at 6 a.m. and lights out at 9 p.m., we were exhausted!

Then came the Selection Board where we had to choose from a list of occupations. I chose cinematography since I had been trained in photography, or Signals. Instead I was given a test in mechanics, and had to assemble a model with pieces of metal and tiny screws within my fat fingers, in a certain time. I failed miserably. Then a written test which was a kind of IQ test with lots of diagrams, I didn't do so badly at this, but had no idea what it was all leading to until called in to see the officer.

I stood to attention and saluted (as taught) and she asked me to sit down. Then informed me that I had been selected to go to driving school. I was dumbfounded, knowing what a mess I had made of the mechanical test, and said so. "But," she said "you excelled in the written test, and that is what matters most."

There were twelve of us selected to go to driving school, twelve very apprehensive but excited young women. None of us had ever driven before, but the officer who accompanied us on the train told us the training would be extensive, and would include mechanics as well as driving, map reading and the usual drill and long distance runs. The training center was at Camberly in Surrey, a beautiful little town where Sandhurst is located: the British equivalent of West Point.

We were re-issued with soft caps, and wore our cap-straps over the top. This is a relic of World War I when nurses rode horseback to the front and wore their cap-straps up, so that they could be easily pulled down under their chins. We were also issued battle-dress and slacks, and hip-length leather jerkins, and much smarter rain-coats.

Inspections at Camberly were rigid, we had to wear hair nets, even with hair as short as mine, to keep our hair off our collars. Drill was Guards Drill, very precise synchronized drill, like the guards do at Buckingham Palace, and every day.

Lectures began immediately, as did mechanics, so we learned how an internal combustion engine worked, first of all on paper, then on real engines.

Driving instruction was on 15 CWT trucks, not just manual gear shift, but double-declutching, which means accelerating between each gear shift as it goes into neutral. A great deal to learn, but what training!

We spent ten weeks at Camberly. The training took place on the grounds of a large beautiful house the army had requisitioned, and next door at another large beautiful house, the present Queen, then Princess Elizabeth, also trained as a driver. She was an officer though, we were just privates!

At the end of the ten weeks came our test, both written and practical. It included reversing around a tight S-bend, stopping on a hill, holding the vehicle still using the clutch and the accelerator, no brakes, and starting again smoothly without stalling, not an easy thing to do on manual. But the worst test was when we had to stop on a hill, the testing officer got out and put a matchstick under the rear wheel. If that matchstick was broken when we drove uphill, we failed our test. I think we were given an extra chance but only one.

Our passing-out parade was a very ceremonial affair where we were presented with our badges, little driving wheels to be sewn on our sleeves.

Ten marvelous weeks where we were congratulated, and told that we should be very proud of ourselves. And we were!

Army Driver

My driving career began after that, first in Nottingham in the center of England, where I was a "pool driver". Each morning our assignments were posted in the orderly office, which car we would be driving, and which officer we were to drive, never the same. We had to be properly dressed in full uniform, hats on, open the car door, salute, and drive wherever our assignments were. Early on, our officers were pretty lenient because we were new drivers. Two of us were posted to Nottingham and Louie and I remained friends all our lives.

For two weeks Louie and I had to go to a maintenance center, and spent eight hours each day in a pit underneath a car or truck, greasing and cleaning, and under the hood taking the carburator apart, cleaning the plugs, and putting it all back together, hoping the car would start.

We rotated the tires, changed the oil, checked the battery and filled it with distilled water, and I'll tell you, by the end of that exhausting two weeks, we knew everything there was to know about engines. I don't think I ever worked so hard, and at the end of it, the vehicle was inspected inside and out, and woe betide you if anything was left dirty or out of place.

After three months as a "pool driver" I applied for a posting, and was transferred to Buntingford, a small village in Hertfordshire, north of London. Beautiful countryside, a village with old, old, buildings, thatched cottages, and thirteen pubs!

This time I drove trucks, except on rare occasions when the Commanding Officer needed his car and his regular driver was away or on leave. Otherwise my uniform became the slacks, battledress and leather jerkin I had been issued with at Camberly. Some of the trucks were 3 Tonners, but mostly I drove Chevrolet 15 CWT trucks with flat fronts, wooden steering wheels, and the engines inside the cabs, nice in the winter to keep you warm. At that time there were no automatic turn signals, or brake lights, so the window had to be rolled down and you used hand signals. I had to have one cushion to sit on and two behind my back in order to reach the pedals because I am quite small. They all called me "Half Pint"!

At this time there were a great many men coming back from overseas where they had taken part in the final battles before the war ended. They were rough, tough, battle-scarred men, but at no time did any of us have cause to be afraid. They were polite and courteous to all of us young girls.

We were six drivers at Buntingford, altogether in the same hut, and took it in turns to be Duty Driver when you were on-call twenty four hours, with the Duty Truck parked outside the hut. We were all required to be able to drive anything and everything they gave us, and go anywhere all over the country carrying parts for vehicles, guns and ammunitions, and men. We had some German POW's working at the workshops, and I was often assigned to drive them back to their camp at the end of the day. One of them with bright red hair used to give me little love notes I remember. I wonder what became of him?

Life was pretty good at Buntingford, there were days when we had to drive long distances, and came back late at night, but there were dances every Saturday evening and free time at weekends.

Some weekends though, I had a pass and took the little train to London to meet up with Anthony who was stationed at Aldershot, an army town. We would go to the NAAFI Club at Leicester Square, to get free tickets for a theater, or try to get in to see Glenn Miller and his band. That was pretty impossible, so we would go round to the back of the theater, and listen to the band through the walls. There was always a crowd there, and we'd dance in the street.

There came the time though, when the services were being discharged, and it was decided to close the women's army section at Buntingford and we were all to be re-posted to other camps.

This time I was sent to Ashford in Kent, it was a sad day when we all left Buntingford for the last time. Saying goodbye to old friends is never easy. Three of us went to Ashford, which was also an Engineering Department of the Army so I drove trucks again, and the occasional staff car.

The winter of 1946 was a mini ice-age. It was terribly cold and there was a lot of snow. Most camps sent their ATS home, but for some reason Ashford didn't. The chains on my truck wheels wore out and snapped, and we had to drain our radiators every night. No antifreeze in those days. There was no heat in our hut, an icicle hung in one corner for six weeks, nothing to burn in our little potbelly stove until I took my truck over to the officers' mess in the dead of night to steal coal. I wasn't caught!

We would line up with our hot water bottles outside the orderly office where there was an electric kettle, and each of us in turn filled our bottles. In the morning, that same water was used for washing ourselves.

We drivers were issued with extra slacks and socks because we were out all the time in the weather, and couldn't dry the ones we were wearing. We put newspapers between the springs of our beds and the mattresses, and also were issued with American quilts left behind when they went home. They were a blessing. It was a very hard winter and I don't know how we all stayed well, but we did. I don't think Britain has had such a winter since 1946.

Again my time in Ashford was coming to an end as more and more army camps were closing. I had one more posting as my own discharge was approaching. So I was sent to Northern Ireland and traveled to Belfast by train to Liverpool, and thence by ferry across the Irish Sea to Ireland.

This last camp was at Lisburn, a permanent British army camp. Just a big brick building with no character at all. I missed the barrack huts, I missed the friends I had made in those other much smaller camps at Buntingford and Ashford. This was a Signals camp and my driving was mostly taking engineers around the countryside repairing telephone wires. Except for the beautiful countryside, it was not a very interesting time. Finally in September 1947 I packed my kit bag for the last time and boarded the ferry in Belfast. Back across the Irish Sea to Liverpool, I took the train to York where I was to be discharged. An insignificant little Army headquarters, a salute to the officer at the desk, I received my last pay packet and demobilization papers, a "Thank you for your service", a handshake, and that was the end.

I had loved my army career, it had turned a young girl with no self-esteem into a self-assured young woman willing to accept responsibility, and it made me who I am today. The training I received at driving school was better than any college, it was in fact, my college degree, and I've been grateful for it all my life. I know I am an exceptionally good driver because of that training.

I have been profoundly influenced by the time I spent in the British Women's Army. Everyone should have that opportunity.

JEAN BARRINGER - Driver in the ATS (Auxiliary Territorial Service) in England during World War II and at Nanton Museum (Alberta, Canada), right, in 2007 with a similar truck.

The Veteran

Told to me by an ex-soldier in 1946
Just after World War II

I'm a veteran my girl
home after fighting overseas
these past six years.
How we would talk
all of us,
how we would long
for the day
the war would end
and we could
all come home.
Where we would eat
proper food
instead of army rations.
Steaks and fish and chips,
fresh bread and butter
not margarine,
and eggs and bacon.
It's been so long
and what do I find my girl?
Nowhere to live
houses bombed,
food still rationed.
No steaks at all,
no butter
no eggs or bacon,
even clothes are rationed.
And no jobs
for returning
servicemen.
Nothing like
the GI Bill
in America.
I lean on my broom
and stare blankly
across the street
I'm supposed
to be sweeping.
The only job
I could find my girl.
Look at me,
It's cold, and I'm wearing
my old army greatcoat.
the buttons are dull,

I don't have to polish
them anymore.
Look at my boots
my girl,
dirty and worn through.
There was a time
when I stood erect my girl,
my boots polished
pants pressed
buttons shining,
I was so proud
of who I was my girl.
and proud
of what I fought for.
I catch sight of myself
in a shop window,
my hair is long
and uncombed
I am bent
and shabby.
The respect I once had for myself
is gone.

The Uncovering

It was over, the war was finally over. After 6 years, this horrible conflict that had destroyed so many lives on both sides had come to an end. There was no winning or losing, just a lot of shattered countries to rebuild and make whole again. But for the moment we had to set everything aside and allow ourselves to rejoice.

In a frenzy we tore down the black-out curtains, and peeled the strips of sticky paper off the windows where they had been criss-crossed on the glass to prevent shattering if a bomb fell close by, and then we turned on the lights. All over town lights were shining in every window, and we all cried.

My sister and I went door to door collecting wooden and cardboard boxes, anything that would burn, and together with the neighbors, stacked it all into a giant pile, and when darkness fell we lit a huge fire. People came from all the streets around and we joined hands and made a circle and danced and sang and cried some more until there was no more fire, and then we went home.

It was so quiet. None of us could believe how quiet it was. The sky was full of stars, there were no searchlights sweeping the sky, no flashes from the big guns, no air raid sirens, there was just silence.

We looked out over the city and there were lights everywhere, the black-out was gone, we could see to walk, there were streetlights, it was a shock, almost too much to take in all at once.

Then at bedtime a real bed to sleep in. Sheets and blankets, not sitting crouched in an air raid shelter all night, or lying under the dining room table, or in the hall closet where there was no glass, we actually undressed and got into bed, and would you believe, couldn't sleep because of the softness of the mattress, and the silence. The silence was overwhelming.

We were so tired of years of not being able to sleep peacefully in our beds.

We were so tired of shortages, and making do with so little, with wearing patched and mended and passed on clothes.

So tired of pretending that all would be well, it was just a matter of time. We were all just so very tired.

Wars are devastating and futile but that war had to be fought, and those of us who were there will never forget the suffering that had to be endured because of it.

The men came home from overseas expecting jobs and homes for themselves and their families, and good food after having to eat army rations for so long, but there was nothing to come home to. We were a shattered broken country with nothing to offer. The reality was devastating.

Australia, New Zealand and Canada came to the rescue and offered cheap fares by sea to each of their countries, along with the promise of jobs and homes. Thousands accepted, and left their country for which they had fought so hard, to make their lives far across the sea, and some never returned.

Anthony and I, young marrieds, also left in 1954 as soon as he had completed his PhD and had been offered a job in Canada. There was no alternative.

It was twelve years before we were able to return, and we felt like strangers, we didn't belong anymore, we had become Canadians, and proudly so.

Britain had become a country of immigrants. After the war when so many of us left, people from Pakistan and the West Indies streamed in to take our places. As in years gone by, populations change, minorities become majorities, customs change, traditions die, new ones are formed. Resentments arise, sometimes there is violence, but nothing ever remains the same.

No Going Back

When Anthony and I were first married we lived on the equivalent of a GI Bill grant and my rather meager salary, and our vacations were spent Youth Hosteling in various parts of England, Scotland and Wales. These were primitive and very cheap, hidden in remote areas where you had to get there "under your own steam" that was the rule. Either hike, bicycle, or canoe. You bought your own food in the nearest village, cooked your own meals and were given a chore to do before you left in the morning.

Sleeping quarters were in a dorm, rough blankets were provided, but you had to bring a sheet sleeping bag or rent one.

Here you met young people from all over the world, equally poor, exchanged stories, got to know them, drifted off next morning, and quite often met up again at another Youth Hostel somewhere else.

One such trip, not having enough funds for the rail fare, we hitch-hiked to Wales, a lovely small mountainous country on the Western side of Britain where the people are miners, devout chapel-goers, romantic poets like Dylan Thomas, actors, brass band enthusiasts, rugby players and known world-wide for their choral singing.

Hard-working, small, dark, they had similar features (you could never mistake a Welshman) and were very suspicious of strangers. The curtain would twitch as you walked by with your packs on your backs, but so welcoming in the little pubs and village stores with their sing-song lilting Welsh voices.

We were heading that day for a Youth Hostel called Roman Bridge, and boarded a country bus full of chattering women speaking mostly in Welsh, a Celtic language, on the decline in the past, but now being revived in the schools.

We asked to be put off at the road to Roman Bridge and were immediately deluged by directions. "Down the long valley, at the very end it is, an old chapel it is, look-you".

The rain began to fall as we got off the bus, and continued as we plodded down that long, long valley. Waves of fine rain enveloped us and seeped through our boots and our rather inadequate rain gear, soaking us through. We could feel and hear our socks squelching as we walked.

We had to pick up the key from a cottage, and found our way to the old chapel building. The door creaked as we pushed it open revealing a small space, bare wooden floor, pointed church windows, but no stained glass in this non-conformist plain society, and rafters criss crossing above supporting the roof. A large fireplace had been added and partitions divided this bare space into sleeping rooms and in the small vestibule a stack of firewood, thankfully dry.

We soon made a fire which sputtered and sparked with the scent of pine resin and blazed into life, warming us through. I heated some canned soup on the oil stove and we stripped off our wet clothes and hung them on chairs in front of the fire.

Another couple arrived soon after, on bicycles, equally wet and hungry, an American couple on their honeymoon.

We had a very interesting and happy evening swapping stories, but next morning we found the mountain streams had swollen and a flood surrounded the building so we were marooned and forced to stay where we were until the water went down. Another day as it happened.

So then we tidied up, swept the floor, cleared the ashes and set the fire for next hostlers, said our good-byes, and set off in different directions. Our route was over the mountain to Blaenau Ffestiniog, a little mining town, and beyond.

Many years later we returned to Wales this time in a rental car, and retraced our journey down the valley to Roman Bridge.

It took a long time to find the chapel but after much backing and forthing, we did. Overgrown bushes and long grass and weeds surrounded it, but there was our sad little chapel.

The roof had fallen in, the door wouldn't open, but we peered through the dirty broken windows at what had been such a warm and welcoming refuge all those years ago.

In hindsight you know, I realize it's never a good idea to go back.

Our Corner of London

In the years between 1948 and 1954, Anthony and I, just married, lived in the part of London between Chelsea, Fulham and Kensington. A curious mixture of red brick Victorian terrace homes, built originally for returning World War I veterans, now occupied by artisans and shopkeepers, and bombed remains of what had once been elegant 19th Century townhouses for the rich, now turned into flats and bed sitting rooms for young couples like us.

Bustling little neighborhoods abounded. It was like a lot of small towns bordering each other in the one gigantic city of London. Bakeries, hardware stores, butchers, fishmongers, and green grocers with their produce outside on trays. Colorful vegetables, fruit, and rows of silver herrings just in from the North Sea, and inevitably the corner fish and chip shop smelling deliciously of frying fish and chips. Neighbors knew each other. Moms wheeled their babies in high English prams, and safely left the babies outside on the street while they did their daily shopping.

Washing was hung on clotheslines in tiny backyards where flowers struggled to grow. Dogs roamed free and left their poop on cracked pavements, and cats yowled to each other at night.

London 'bobbies' (policemen) strolled leisurely along their beats, hands behind their backs and greeting everyone with a smile, not a gun to be seen. Bobbies were everybody's best friends, holding the hands of children to escort them safely across the street on their way to school and they were always there to point directions to strangers in London for the first time.

Evidence of the recent wartime bombing was everywhere, the debris cleared away, but sides of bombed houses were visible as if sliced in half by a giant cake knife. The slanting remnants of staircases leading up two or three stories, and the square holes which had been fireplaces. Nothing left of what once had been cherished homes.

The patches of waste ground where homes had been, but now untidy grass grew and the bright pink spires of willow herb flourished. There also the children played without thought of the devastation only a few years before.

These close-knit little communities grew out of shared war experiences and the determination to repair and renew our lives, put all that behind us, look towards the bright future for our children and "make it happen".

The Market on The North End Road

Every Saturday I took the red double-decker bus to the street market on the North End Road. People from all walks of life flocked there, all came by bus. Nobody had cars in 1950.

The market stretched for about half a mile along the busy dusty London street.

Cockney vendors stood behind their vegetable carts, shouting their wares in the very broad Cockney dialect, all the produce was tempting and a riot of color amidst the tall grey soot-covered buildings.

The prices varied, some better than others, so I never bought from the first stall, but slowly walked the length of the street weaving my way through the crowds of noisy shoppers, comparing prices, carrying a large deep orange basket over each arm.

The vegetables I bought had to last a week, and I only had a limited amount of money to spend, everything I earned went on food, nothing left over.

I stopped to buy tomatoes, little English ones, so sweet and tender, reaching to select the ripe red ones on display, only to be shouted at by the stall owner. 'Ere, he said, "You can't take those, they're just for display those are," and what he gave me came from behind, the ones that were bruised and certainly inferior. He put them in a bag, swung it over to twist the ends, and took my money. The scales were behind, too, they were a crafty lot, those Cockneys.

Further along the street, mushroom stalks were the equivalent of 5 cents a pound. The mushroom caps went to the hotels, but the stalks were a good meal for two with our ration of bacon and tomatoes, so I bought a pound for supper that night. Carrots still with dirt on them, not scrubbed clean, a small dark green cabbage, runner beans that are sliced length-wise. Not peas, though, because they have to be shelled and pods weigh a lot You didn't get many peas out of a pound.

New potatoes, from the Channel Islands, small with skins that could be rubbed off with the thumb, so tender were they, and cooking apples called Bramley Seedlings bursting with vitamin C.

My baskets were full now, and heavy. I stopped to count my money, enough for a crusty baguette. I had smelled them baking on the way down the road. I splurged and bought two and tucked them one under each arm.

I made my way back to the bus stop and boarded the bus when it came. It was full of shoppers similarly laden, and I had to stand, there were no seats. It wasn't far to my stop, but I still had a long way to walk with loaded baskets.

Anthony and I lived in two rooms on the top floor of an old London house. Slowly I climbed the fifty stairs to the top and let myself into our small flat, thinking how lucky we were to have each other, and a place to live, and wonderful fruit and vegetables from the street market at the North End Road.

Washing Day in Raphael Street

I remember washing day in the '40's when we were first married, and lived in two rooms at the top of an 18th Century house in the middle of London.

There was nothing romantic about living in an 18th Century house, which had two rooms on each of the three floors, and the kitchen in the basement.

Five people shared the kitchen, which we had patched and sealed, scrubbed clean and painted. We all ate there too, five members of the same family, including my mother-in-law. It wasn't always easy, but we were lucky in those days of bombed buildings to find anywhere to live at all.

Anthony was at college, and I worked for a theatrical photographer. We bicycled to school and work to save money, and took our lunch, and were able to meet in the park right by the Albert Hall. In a way it was idyllic.

Except for washing day!

Each of us had to wash on separate days because there was only one sink. I would put everything in to soak in the morning, sprinkle with soap flakes and go to work.

There it would sit, a congealed grey mass of wet clothes, until I could get around to it after supper.

I don't know anyone who had a washing machine, let alone a dryer in those days. In Britain after the war, we had washboards and Sunlight soap, and elbow grease.

I remember standing over that sink after a day's work rubbing the clothes on the washboard until my knuckles were raw, and oh, how my back ached!

There was no hot water from the faucets, so we boiled kettles on the stove two at a time, and kept scrubbing, dropping each item into a bucket, then rinsing several times, wringing by hand, and finally pegging it outside on a line in the small courtyard.

If we were lucky it wasn't raining, but if it was, then everything would have to be hung on an indoor rack and hoisted to the ceiling and left to dry. The drying could take all week because there was no heat in the house, and then of course it had to be ironed!

These are my memories of washing day in the 40s. Now, I never put a wash in the machine without giving it a grateful pat. Never, never, do I take it, or my dryer for granted, and sometimes I think we need to go through periods of hardship in order to appreciate the good things in life.

Just a House

The stone house stood
in a quiet street
large, imposing,
surrounded by green lawns
bordered by rhododendrons
ten feet high
ablaze with magenta blooms.

Ornate iron railings
and the creaking
squeaking gate
led through
the gravel path
to the front door.

Once long ago,
more than 100 years ago,
the house stood alone,
with even wider lawns,
an orchard at the side,
and beds of fragrant flowers.

My father
bought this granite house
handed my mother the key
large, ornate, it was
this key from long ago,
twisted in the lock,
the door
heavy and black
swung open.

A tiled lobby,
a wide paneled hall.
My mother caught her breath
visions of grandeur
overwhelmed her,
"lady of the manor"
she thought
as she stepped
into the house.
Long empty
thick with dust,
the curving staircase
glowing wood
climbed to the second floor.

One by one
the rooms
lay before her.
Carved cornices,
graceful windows,
heavy oaken doors.
A kitchen
with its black wood stove
bells with coils
ready to summon
servants to their chores.

All this, a bygone age,
a long ago time.
No servants now
to answer bells
or stoke the fires.
No gardener
to mow the lawns
prune the apple trees
plant the beds
touch his cap
and call her Ma'am
But oh that house!
Cold as the grave.
Ice on the windows
scraped with the thumb
ice-reforming
walls so thick,
the cold seeped in
and never got out.

It was just a house,
a cold, cold house
never a home.

The Voyage of "The Inver"

It was 1952, and my husband Tony was a graduate student at the Royal School of Mines in London, while I worked as a technician in a photographic studio.

Every summer, Tony was required to do his field work on mining properties as part of his course, and that year he was completing his graduate studies at the Rio Tinto mine in Southern Spain.

As a very magnanimous gesture, I was invited to spend the summer with him. The Rio Tinto mine was owned by a British Company, and a large group of British men and their wives and families lived and worked there. We were to live at the Company Guest House in the community.

I was to travel by the Company ship, "The Inver", a small cargo ship which sailed regularly via the Manchester Ship Canal to Huelva in southern Spain. I took the train from London to Manchester in the central part of England, and made my way to the shipping office. Tony was already in Spain, so I was on my own and more than a little nervous. I was looking forward to the voyage because I knew that cargo ships could be quite luxurious, and I imagined that a large mining company such as Rio Tinto would have such a ship.

When I reached the office, I was introduced to Captain Brines, an Irishman, dressed in a regular suit and peaked cap, not a uniform as I expected. I discovered at that point that the company vessel was not legally supposed to carry passengers and I had to be signed on as 3rd mate. I began to have misgivings. What kind of a ship was this? What was a 3rd mate supposed to do, I became intrigued and a little uneasy, and more so as time went on.

They called a taxi, my luggage loaded, and I was driven out of Manchester towards the Manchester Ship Canal. This waterway has been in existence for more than a hundred years and was, and is the main route for cargo-carrying barges, and shipping from the center of England to the sea.

Suddenly the driver pulled off the road onto a gravel track, and after about a mile, stopped the car and got out "Oh my God, what now?" I thought. He shouldered my luggage, "Follow me" he said, and strode up a little incline, and there at the bottom of the bank was the dirtiest, grimiest little rust-bucket of a ship I had ever set eyes upon! The smart luxurious cargo ship disappeared in a flash. My cargo ship was a collier! It transported coal from England to the Rio Tinto Mine, and brought back ore.

I stepped gingerly onto a plank of wood that served as a gang-plank, over some coils of greasy rope, across a deck thick with soot and coal dust to be greeted by the 1st mate, and shown to my cabin which was a small room on a level with the deck. It contained two bunks about 30" wide, one fore and aft, and the other sideways on, each had wooden side rails. There was a closet, and a tiny wash-basin in the corner. No shower, no toilet, which I was to discover was down a metal ladder in the engine room. The stokers, incidentally were

71

all Arabs. "How" I thought "would I negotiate that ladder when this little ship was butting through the high seas?" I was hardly dressed for this kind of sea voyage, a wool skirt and sweater was just about all I had to wear until we got to warmer climes. Pants would have been much more suitable, but women didn't wear pants much in those days, and I didn't possess any anyway.

I stowed my clothes in the closet, washed my face and hands, which I was to discover would always be dirty, and went back outside. "Never lock your cabin door" said the 1st mate and led me to the dining room where I was introduced to the rest of the crew. They were all Irishmen it turned out, half from the South and other half from the North. It was obviously going to be an interesting trip! Indeed it was, they argued and fought back and forth all the way to Spain. The exception was the 2nd mate, another Irishman in his 80's who had his Master's ticket in sail. He also maneuvered to sit beside me at meals, told the most outrageous stories, and pinched my knees under the table!

"Remember" said Captain Brines "don't lock your cabin door". "Like Hell" I thought thinking of the fighting Irishmen, and the lecherous 2nd mate! The reason for the Captain's instructions became obvious though. In high seas, the decks could be swamped, and so could my cabin. Someone would have to get in to rescue me, and this actually happened to the previous passenger.

That evening, we left Manchester and chugged slowly along the Canal towards the River Mersey and Liverpool, and by nightfall reached the Irish Sea. I could tell immediately when that happened, the Irish Sea is notoriously rough, and the ship began to pitch a bit against the waves, The engine increased and we picked up speed, and through the night I could feel that wild sea, and hung onto the rail of my bunk to stop myself falling out. I wasn't sick but I did feel decidedly queasy! Next morning though, at breakfast, the teasing began. I knew that Barbara, the passenger before me, had not been seasick, and so I had to lie through my teeth to uphold our reputation.

As we sailed beyond the Irish Sea, it quietened down a bit, I could see the rugged rocks of the Cornish coast as we made our way into the English Channel, and thought about all the other ships in history that had passed that way. The Spanish Galleons in the Armada that came to fight the English at the time of the first Elizabeth, and the hundreds of vessels large and small that had crossed the Channel only a few years before to invade Normandy on D-Day.

I was put to work sweeping decks, polishing brasses, and even steering the ship, leaving a very crooked wake indeed. I began to find my sea-legs and was beginning to enjoy this very different kind of voyage. As we approached the Bay of Biscay, that great stretch of ocean from North America all the way to France and Portugal, the mighty Atlantic rollers took our little ship. We began to lift and sink, pitch and toss. Biscay also has a reputation for big seas, not rough, as much as huge smooth rolling waves.

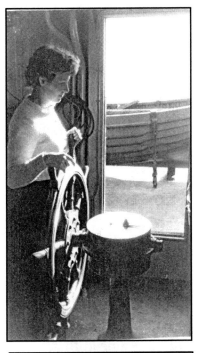

I found that washing myself was quite an adventure. With no shower it meant washing down in that very tiny wash basin. I had to spread newspapers on the floor because with one foot in the bowl, balancing on the other, the ship would roll, and the water would spill over the rim all over the floor. Coal dust was everywhere, so everything was dirty. It was a losing battle.

There were eight pairs of twinkly Irish eyes at all meals as they watched me, comparing me, I thought, to the exemplary Barbara, but I didn't let her down!

Southward we went into the sunshine, leaving the cool foggy British weather behind. In the distance I could see the hazy coast of Portugal, and then as we got closer, Lisbon and on the cliff above, the white Castle of St. George, and rounded into the Mediterranean preceded by shoals of dolphins. How clear and sparkling the water was, and how blue and green.

Very soon we entered Spanish waters and sailed up the River Tinto to the port of Huelva. There stood the giant sculpture of Christopher Columbus, pointing towards the Atlantic and the New World. Huelva was the port from which he had sailed in 1492. We dropped anchor in the river and out from the dock came a little launch with my husband Tony on board. I was so excited to be with him again.

I said good-bye to the Inver and to Captain Brines, and to all my Irish friends who had taken such good care of me, and climbed down the rope ladder to the launch, completely forgetting in my excitement, to sign off as 3rd mate at the shipping office. In consequence, I'm afraid I had to be declared as a deserter!

Immigration - The Journey

I walked out onto the tarmac with my four-month-old baby in my arms. The airplane that was to carry us to Canada stood waiting, and it didn't look big enough to be flying such a distance. "A Constellation" they told me, not even a Super Constellation which was a larger model of the same plane. It was 6 p.m. on a dark cold evening, March 2, 1954, and I was travelling alone, my husband having gone ahead of me a month earlier, and this was my first flight.

I wasn't nervous, but very excited, it was an adventure. The flight attendant took us on ahead of the other passengers because of the baby, up the metal staircase and onto the aircraft. I was seated at the rear of the plane along with a young couple who also had a baby. There weren't many other passengers I remember, I suppose it wasn't the best time of year to be flying to Canada, but it didn't occur to me that it was still winter, and there could be weather issues, I didn't even think about it.

The other passengers boarded, the doors closed and the captain announced that our first stop for refueling would be Keflavic, Iceland. I looked out at the lighted terminal buildings of Prestwick Airport, situated west of Glasgow on the west coast of Scotland. We trundled out onto the runway, and turned around at the far end. One by one the four engines were tested, and then very slowly the plane moved down the runway gathering speed as it went. I saw the lights of the airport as we passed them, and then they were gone.

I felt the aircraft lift into the air, and kind of hesitate for a moment, before the engines took us up into and through the clouds into a starlit sky. I wished it had been daylight so that I could see where we were. I knew we would be passing over the beautiful Western Isles, the Inner and Outer Hebrides, on the way to Iceland, but all I could see were the stars and the wing with the lights flashing on the end.

After a couple of hours we began to descend, and I could see the lights below. Keflavic had been an American airbase during World War II, and we were told we would be landing and that all passengers would be required to disembark while we refueled, all except the babies, and the stewardess would remain on board to care for them. I didn't much care for that idea, but that's how it was.

As we all went down the staircase to the tarmac, we were met by the most intense cold I had ever encountered. Snow was blowing across the tarmac in a ground blizzard, and I was glad then that I wasn't carrying Christopher through that wind and cold. The airport building was a Quonset hut, the remnant of the old airbase, a large bare hut with trestle tables and benches, but warm and welcoming, and they gave us hot chocolate and cookies while we waited. Around us on the walls were torn posters, photographs of pin-up girls like Betty Grable, Dorothy Lamour and Lana Turner, and boards with signatures of the airmen who only a few years ago were based there. Crews of the air-rescue planes, Cansoes, or

PBY's which flew out over the North Atlantic, patrolling the convoys, ever watchful for the U-boats on the prowl. It was a strange spooky feeling to be there, full of the ghosts of the young men who had called Keflavic home during World War II.

After a while we were called to re-board, and once again, the engines were started, taking time to warm up in that cold air, all four propellers were tested one after another, and we took off and headed west.

The baby was fine all this time tucked up in his little cocoon of blankets. I fed him and he slept again. I didn't sleep at all, I sat and watched the stars as they rocked up and down, up and down.

How would it be in Canada? I was going first to Montreal where I would be staying with friends for a week before travelling on to Toronto. Anthony was already working as a field-geologist in Northern Ontario, and would be flown out by bush plane in order to meet me and get me settled, before returning to the bush.

I must have slept because it was sometime later that I felt the plane bank and swing to the south. Once more we were to land to refuel, this time in Gander, Newfoundland, and as the headlights switched on I could see the snow blowing past. We landed on a very bumpy runway, I don't think it could have been used very much in 1954. The lights showed a few hangars and huts, this was the airport then.

We were allowed to take the babies with us this time, and made our way through a canyon of snow, towering way above our heads. The airport workers wore parkas with fur-lined hoods, and bright checked jackets and hats with ear flaps. Canadians looked so very different from Brits. I realized that neither of us had clothes that were suitable for that cold climate. It would have to be my first priority.

Inside the warm hut we were given hot coffee and ham sandwiches, and I was able to get some warm water to make Christopher's formula, and then we were back on the airplane and on our way to Montreal.

Still another four hours to go, but then it turned into five hours and five and a half, as we circled Montreal in a blizzard. Finally at 6 am we landed, and I carried my screaming baby through the snow. There was Immigration to go through, and baggage to claim and then I found, nobody to meet me!

The people at TransCanada Airlines as it was then, were kindness itself, they took care of everything. They gave me a private room to sit while I changed and fed the baby, gave me hot tea and scrambled eggs, and then phoned my friend Eileen to say I had arrived. I had not thought that of course she couldn't meet me, 6 am, and she also had a young child, and no car. And so it was, that TCA got me a taxi and sent me on my way.

As we drove out onto the highway, we had to stop at a railroad crossing while the biggest locomotive I had ever seen, came slowly by, bell clanging, snowplow on the front, and Canadian Pacific in large letters on the side. This giant train went by, I'm sure for my benefit, many huge cars, and finally a caboose. It couldn't have been a more fitting introduction to the country I had come to.

My friends' apartment was modest, but comfortable, outside the temperature was down near zero, but that little apartment was so warm. I keep mentioning that word "warm", and I think that the warmth of the buildings I went into is what impressed me more than anything else. I had come from a country where houses were so cold inside, one small fireplace heated one room, the rest of the house was ice cold. In fact there were icicles hanging from the bathroom faucets all winter. Everybody suffered from chilblains, a form of frostbite. Fingers and toes became red and swollen, itched and burned, then broke and bled. I remember not being able to hold a pencil at school, my fingers were so swollen. There in Montreal, in that glorious warmth, my swollen chilblains disappeared in a few days.

Eileen took me to a supermarket, we didn't have supermarkets in Britain at that time, and I simply stood in the doorway and stared in amazement at all the food on display. In Britain food was still rationed in 1954, I don't remember ever seeing this amount of food. Long display cases of meat, cut and packaged; eggs, butter and cheese; bottles of milk in refrigerators; and shelves packed with tea and coffee, jams and canned fruit and the displays of fruit and vegetables astounded me. I couldn't take it all in, there was so much.

These people, these Canadians looked so different from the people I had left behind. They had color in their cheeks, the children were round and healthy, the young people tall, muscular and bright eyed. How different it all was! But it was the happy laughter that I remember most. Canadians had jobs, and their own homes with their own kitchens and bathrooms, they didn't have to share. They had refrigerators and washing machines, some had dryers even, and a lot of them had cars.

They didn't know about, or understand what life was like in Europe, how could they possibly understand?

I knew then, that I was ready to live in this happy country, adopt new ways and accept whatever life had in store for me, and life, as I was about to find out, had a great many obstacles lying in wait for me.

A week later, a taxi took Christopher and me to the airport for the flight to Toronto. We boarded a "North Star", which turned out to be a rickety old aircraft left over from goodness knows when, but I was much too interested in the landscape I was flying over to notice the bumps.

Along the St. Lawrence River, still ice bound, across the rolling snow-covered border country of Southern Ontario with small towns dotting the countryside. The shores of Lake Ontario and finally the massed buildings of Toronto.

In 1954, Toronto was not the huge prosperous city it is now, and the airport was a few hangers and two little Quonset huts. Amazing when I think of the giant terminal buildings there now. The plane landed on a bumpy runway, and rolled to a stop. I could see the two huts, and some cars parked on a small unpaved parking lot. Where was Anthony? I suddenly had horrible misgivings that he wouldn't be there, maybe held up in the bush because of weather.

I was last off the plane, and helped by the stewardess, I made my way across the snow-packed ground, and there he was. A fellow geologist had driven him to meet me, and he looked every inch a Canadian in a red and black checked coat and a hat with fur ear flaps.

Thinking back now, I realize that I had come to a town, hardly a city, still part of a very rural landscape, but beginning to push out to the north, east and west.

What a different lifestyle this was going to be, but I was ready and eager to open the door and step into a new world.

Remembering

This week I watched a program about veterans, an interview with four returning vets and their feelings then and now. Was it worth the blood and treasure, did we make a difference? How did they feel about returning home? Did they notice a detachment amongst returning veterans and the rest of us who had never been involved in combat? "Only Vietnam vets understood" one said, "nobody here at home could understand the difference between life in Iraq, and the 'real life' here in this country where people have not experienced warfare."

I felt that too when I first emigrated back in 1954 and came to Canada. Nobody had experienced the war first-hand. The cold, the constant bombing, the nights spent in an air-raid shelter waiting for the next wave of planes, the wail of sirens, the whine of bombs, the crashing gunfire close at hand, the lack of sleep, the lining up for rations, the clipping of coupons to get very little food, the lining up for everything in fact.

No pretty clothes to wear when you're young and longing for some color in your lives. The mending and patching of clothes we already had, to make them last just a little while longer, the passing on of children's clothes out grown, but still good, to another child growing up fast. The bond between every citizen, the pulling together of ordinary people. All of us solidly behind Winston Churchill no matter what our political leanings were. He held us together with his speeches when times were the darkest and gave us hope.

America sent over food, dried eggs, dried milk, mashed potato powder and Spam. How we treasured that Spam! We used the dried eggs to make omelettes, and cut up Spam inside them. Occasionally bananas came across the dark Atlantic on Merchant ships and oranges, only for the children though. Little pinched faces starved for the nourishing food they needed.

The blackouts at night, no lights showing at all, how did we see? The rolling power-cuts, depriving us of heat and light.

Yet we survived all these adversities because we knew we must.

Arriving in Canada, a land of warmth and light and plentiful food. Stores stocked with meat and eggs and milk in bottles, stores filled with racks of pretty clothes, young and fresh and full of color. Oh yes it was a different world. Nobody I met could possibly understand what life was like over there. Had not an inkling of the darkness and the drab reality we lived through every day.

Oh yes it was different, the clear-eyed children, the strong and tall young men at high school, their bodies fit and muscular. A different life, a people who laughed a lot, I noticed that particularly, having jobs to go to, cars, and homes of their own, where they didn't have to share a kitchen and bathroom like we did, lucky to have two rooms and passed-on second hand furniture.

And so we came to North America, amazed at what we found, adjusted and became part of it, but never forgetting what we had left behind.

We blessed Canada for opening their arms to us and making us so very welcome. We blessed the U.S. for food they sent that literally saved us, and for sending their young men to fortify a weary Britain, alone so long, a nation broken by war, but never beaten.

Moving On

Being the wife of a geologist was the first lesson I had to learn, and it began a week after I arrived, a new immigrant to Toronto, Canada, in early March 1954.

After a week of getting settled in, Tony left again for the Northern Ontario forest and I wasn't to see him again until July.

It appeared that geologists and prospectors worked in the bush looking for new mines, between "freeze up and break up", when for a few short weeks they come back to civilization, weatherbeaten, grizzled and smelling of wood smoke.

For those who don't know what "freeze up and break up" means, it is the times of the year when the ice on the lakes is forming, or beginning to thaw, so that the small bush planes can't take off or land safely, with either floats or skis. Bush planes are the only way geologists and prospectors can get in or out of the forest areas, and of course the mail and supplies are also brought in this way.

They lived in cabins partially made of logs, with canvas tent tops, heated by small potbelly stoves, and they moved around on long Canadian snowshoes.

It was quite a unique experience for my husband, fresh from the Royal School of Mines in London, but he loved the life, and when he came home for his short breaks, it wasn't long before he was itching to get back again.

For me though, everything in this new country was different and shopping from a catalogue was one of the first things. You simply scanned through the pages of this fat picture book, lifted the phone and ordered. There were no credit cards in those days, you had to pay by check when it was delivered.

And so my baby's "pram" arrived one day, an ugly grey plastic contraption, totally unsuitable for a Canadian winter I thought, with vents everywhere to let in the cold winds. So unlike an English pram constructed of wood, snug and cozy, with a vent-free hood, and apron that protected the baby from the cold.

Well, what came in the Eaton's Department Store delivery truck was what I had to use, and after all, it's what other Canadians used, so it must be alright, I must get used to it, but it was hard not to compare.

The furnished duplex we had rented was a dream come true for me. I didn't have to share a kitchen and bathroom and it even had a refrigerator. It didn't have a washing machine, or a dryer, but then I'd never had a washing machine before, or a dryer, so washing my baby's diapers by hand was no hardship, and neither was hanging them outside on a line. Even if it was below freezing and I had to pry them frozen off the line, they came in smelling of fresh air.

Christopher had grown from an infant into a toddler when Tony came home in July, and we bought a used 1953 Dodge, and had to pass a driving test of course. Driving on the right was new, but now I could get around and explore, and had begun to make new friends.

We had become Canadian citizens that summer, and I knew it wouldn't be long before we would be on the move again and in September, Tony was transferred to New Brunswick in the Maritimes.

So we packed our few belongings into the two steel trunks that had come across the Atlantic with us, and shipped them by rail to the town where we were going to be living, St. Stephen, just across the border of Maine, a sister town in fact, of Calais in Maine.

We left Toronto in our 1953 Dodge, with Christopher in a little canvas baby seat, hooked onto the back of the seat between us. No safety belts then, or safe baby carriers. We decided to travel south via New York City because we wanted to see the famous skyline.

The interstate highway had not been completed in 1954, so we drove most of the way through the state via the byroads and through the delightful small towns and wouldn't have had it any other way. We stayed in cabins which cost an average of $10.00 a night, and we thought that was very expensive indeed!

It was a wonderful experience, especially when we saw the New York City skyline for the first time, drove around Central Park, and went up the Empire State Building.

From New York we then drove north to Boston and on up through Maine to the Canadian border at Calais, over the St. Croix River to our destination, St. Stephen, New Brunswick. It had been a long journey but an enchanting one through the countryside of New England in the fall.

Reaching St. Stephen we found a town in a very bad state of repair, most of the stores boarded up, practically no employment except the chocolate factory Ganongs, which I understand is still there.

The house we were going to be renting belonged to an elderly couple who were going to spend the winter in Florida, but would not be available for another week, and so we had to spend some more time traveling.

It was October and getting quite cold and the Northern Lights spread their waves across the sky. The cabins we stayed in there had hot and cold running water, but not much else. Heat was provided by potbelly stoves, which frequently went out during the night, and the water froze in the pipes so that we would have to go to the office for a can of hot water to wash.

There was not much traffic on the roads of New Brunswick which were back roads anyway, so we didn't have much choice as to where to stay. Our main concern was the baby of course and invariably we took him into bed with us to keep him warm.

To fill in the week before we could move in, we drove north to the town of Bathurst where there happened to be a staking rush going on. The town was crowded with prospectors invading the bars and having a high old time before going off into the bush to stake claims.

We stayed in an old red brick Victorian Hotel for a couple of nights, much more comfortable than a cabin, meeting up for dinner with a group of the Selection Trust prospectors in town for the staking.

It was all very new and exciting for a couple of Brits straight from the Old Country. Tony had been initiated already, having worked in the bush for the past 7 months, but for me, this was like a movie.

After a week, we returned to St. Stephen and met our hosts. We were to spend the winter in that little house, and what a winter it was! I had bought a red parka with a fur hood for myself, from the catalogue, and a snowsuit for Christopher. Runners that could be attached to the wheels of the baby carriage for use in snow, and so much snow there was! Feet of it piled in drifts in front of the garage, a lot of heavy digging when Tony had to use the car to visit various camps around.

We had to have a block heater to keep the radiator from freezing overnight, in fact everyone had a block heater. The temperature went down to -30°F and below, and everything outside cracked and snapped with the cold, including the walls of the house.

We had in the basement, a furnace that looked like a giant spider, with pipes going in all directions. It had been converted from wood-burning to oil only recently, and I found it most intriguing when the oil truck arrived, and plugged a long hose into a connector in the wall. Miraculously this thing with long arms kept us warm all winter long.

Every day, I took the baby out either in the sleigh or baby carriage for a walk, swaddled to the eyebrows in blankets and scarves. We got our groceries from a little corner grocery store, and sometimes that's as far as we went. Other times we walked down to the town and across the bridge into the U.S. The customs officers on both sides of the border got to know us and we got cheerful waves from all of them.

Calais and St. Stephen at that time, were pretty rundown small towns, there was very little employment and a lot of the stores were boarded up. There was however, a very small Penneys on the American side. It had creaky floorboards, and not much in the way of merchandise, but it was from this little Penneys that I bought our towels and sheets, smuggled across the border underneath Christopher!

The two towns shared the one hospital and fire department. All American babies were born in Canada, and all Canadian fires were put out by the American Fire Department.

That was a hard winter, 1954-1955 more snow and cold than I had ever experienced. We spent 6 months in that little border town and it was very hard to leave. The warmth and generosity of the people of St. Stephen is something I will never forget.

Remembering St. Stephen

How could I not write a separate story about St. Stephen, where we spent our first Canadian winter?

It was a little town on the banks of the St. Croix river, and just across the bridge from Calais, Maine. Twin cities they were, only not cities, but small towns, with citizens of both countries living in harmony, and sharing many services like the Hospital and Fire Department.

We rented a small furnished house on the edge of town, whose owners had gone south to Florida for the winter, and what a warm cozy home it was! I had much to learn that first Canadian winter, just how very cold it could be, and how the people prepared by stacking pine branches against the bases of their homes, to keep an insulating space between the branches and the snow when it came, and oh how the snow came!

One day when I was out with Christopher snug in blankets on the sleigh, a fog suddenly swept down the hill and wrapped around us, only it wasn't fog, it was a blizzard such as I'd never seen before, a complete white-out of very fine snow. If we hadn't been close to home, I'd have been lost, but I knew it would have been perfectly alright to have knocked at the door of the closest house, and we would have been taken in.

The roads around town were solid ice, children skated to school, and I had sleigh runners fitted to the wheels of the baby's carriage so that I could get out and walk to town if I needed to. Some delivery vehicles were actually big horse-drawn sleighs.

There was a corner grocery run by Phil and Ann who had a little girl Christopher's age, and it was to Phil's grocery that I usually went for food, but Ann and my other friend, Dorothy Hyslop, a war bride from Scotland, and I, would often go down to town and across the bridge into Calais with our baby carriages "if the wheelin' was good." Calais had a "Penney's" a very small Penney's, with creaky floor boards and not much in the way of merchandise, but I stocked up with sheets and towels, tucked them under the baby, and walked blithely across the bridge, waving to the customs officers who knew darn well we were smuggling.

Both little towns were in dire straits, a lot of the stores boarded up. The only employment in St. Stephen was at Ganongs, the chocolate factory. The textile mill on the river had closed and there was nothing much else.

Once, out for a walk with Christopher I discovered some beautiful old Victorian mansions dating from the time when there was money in the town. All now empty and abandoned, all built of wood, very ornate with lots of gingerbread around large porches, but shutters now broken and banging in the wind. It made me feel very sad to see these lonely old homes, I should have found out more about them.

Dorothy's husband was a customs officer and they lived in a red brick Victorian house with their three little boys. A wood-burning furnace heated the house and had to be stacked with wood before they went to bed so that it would provide enough heat to last all night, but often didn't. All the downstairs rooms had grills in the ceilings, so that warm air could circulate through the house, but Bob invariably had to get up in the night to stack more wood in the furnace.

The temperature went down to -30° and below at night, and the walls of our house would snap with the cold, as did the trees. Tony would have to travel to the prospecting camps in the forest, going as far as he could by car, kept warm all night by a block heater, and then by snow shoes to where the crews were. We all hoped that mineralization would be found so that a mine could be drilled and provide employment for the town, but it wasn't to be.

From the very beginning Tony and I were included in gatherings at neighbors' homes, and at the Canadian Legion where the town held suppers provided by the townsfolk in recognition of the servicemen and women who had served their country in Europe. Tony and I were both ex-service and I remember being very embarrassed when we were required to march into the hall with all the other ex-service people, not knowing a soul. We very soon did though, remember this was 1954, not many years after World War II had ended.

There were many times that winter, when Tony drove our little second-hand 1953 Dodge up to Fredericton and to Bathurst in the northern part of New Brunswick. He would have to stay over if the weather was bad, but most of times he drove home through the snow. I would watch for the car's headlights to appear round the corner, and see the snow slanting in the lights as he drove on the ice up to our driveway. Sometimes it was very late, but he would always telephone to let me know he was on his way. I left all the lights on in the house to guide him home, and have the kettle boiling, and hot soup ready, but it was an anxious time for me when he went on one of his trips. That winter in St. Stephen he was home most of the time though. His job was to supervise the crews already in the bush gathering rock samples, and analyzing them for traces of mineralization.

When Christmas came I made plum puddings and Christmas cake, clinging to the traditions familiar to my British upbringing. We stored the puddings in the shed outside to freeze, but the mice ate all of them but one I'm afraid. The cake, well laced with brandy, we kept in the house sealed in a round cake tin, so the little critters never got to that!

Our Christmas tree was one that had fallen off a delivery wagon, and Tony found it on the road. We didn't have any decorations or lights, but we hung it with Christmas cards, and very pretty it looked too.

There weren't many presents for Christopher that first Christmas. Our folks in Britain didn't realize they had to post Christmas mail in October for it to get to us in time. All mail at that time came by sea-mail across the Atlantic and took a very long time to reach us. We bought a few things for him of course, but being only a year old he didn't really know what he was missing. New Year came and went and there were parties to go to. People made their own entertainment, and got together at every opportunity to celebrate.

The extreme cold and frequent snow-storms lasted well into the New Year, but eventually the days began to lengthen, and warm up, and the snow melt. The farmers set fire to their fields to burn last year's wheat and corn stalks, and the dried-up remains of produce and old grass, to provide nitrogen for the spring planting.

In early April, my mother-in-law (Doe-Doe) arrived from Britain for a visit. She traveled by freighter across the Atlantic, and hers was the first ship to get through the ice on the St. Lawrence that year. The captain was presented with the traditional "gold cane" in honor of the occasion. Great entertainment on board! We drove to Three Rivers, Quebec to meet her and her short visit was to last a year!!

A few weeks later we received news of a transfer up to the north of New Brunswick to Bathurst where mineralization had been found and a staking rush was in progress. Selection Trust was participating of course and sending our prospectors out to stake claims in the bush. So were a lot of other mining companies, and there was a great deal of excitement and anticipation in the town.

We were so sorry to be leaving St. Stephen, especially since we weren't able to find a mine in the area. We knew a lot of the residents had been pinning their hopes on that. This had been our first real introduction to Canadian life in that wonderful little town. How very special those people were!

Late in April we hitched the company trailer to the jeep and Tony left ahead of us, while Doe Doe, Christopher and I drove the blue Dodge out of St. Stephen for the last time. We set out for the next part of our lives in a totally different atmosphere in the French-speaking town of Bathurst. Just how completely different we were soon to discover.

The Little Lost House on the Bay

It was the end of April 1955 when we again packed our belongings, and moved north to the town of Bathurst, New Brunswick. A French-speaking town close to the Quebec border. It was a surprisingly lively little town, and the paper mills provided most of the employment – and the odor!

My mother-in-law had recently arrived from England for a visit, so we set out to look for a furnished rental house in the neighborhood. Tony was going to be working in the bush close by, and although he wouldn't be home all the time, we knew we would be able to see him fairly often.

As a geologist's wife, this picking up and moving on was what I had to do if I were to see my husband at all.

Finding a two or three bedroom furnished house was proving to be difficult, and although I would have preferred living in the town, there was nothing available.

So one cold day we drove north about five miles out of town to Danny's Diner, where a realtor had told us he had a property for rent. Danny led us three miles along a dirt road where ruts were still frozen and puddles filled with ice, and banks of snow remained at the sides of the road and in amongst the trees. Winter comes early, and lingers long in this northern country.

We followed Danny as he turned off the road between two willow trees, onto a track that led to a wooden house, appropriately called "Twin Willows", standing in a field bordering on the flats of the Bay of Chaleur.

It had once been painted red, but there it stood lonely and abandoned, paint peeling, wooden steps broken, and the screen door hanging on one hinge.

I hoisted my baby onto my hip and followed Danny up the wooden steps and into a large kitchen area, dominated by an enormous black iron stove, but little else. It was bare and cold, linoleum on the floor, a wooden table and four chairs, and in the other room, an old red plush chaise was all the furniture there was. This was a furnished house? Upstairs the three bedrooms had beds and chests of drawers and a bathroom, but no water until the thaw.

I looked aghast at that stove, and Danny said, "You'll soon learn" and he pulled open one damper, and pushed another, thrust some sticks into the firebox and lit them and they roared into life, then he added logs and suddenly we had a fire going.

Next he said "Follow me" and taking two buckets went out into the field about 100 yards away, let the buckets down into a hole in the ground and hauled up water. This then was to be our water supply until the weather warmed up and we could turn on the water in the house.

Why we rented that house I'll never know, but we didn't have much choice. There was a staking rush on, the town was full of prospectors and geologists, and mining companies including ours, intent on staking their claims in the bush, and all based in town.

Next to us, in the field stood a large Victorian house soon to be occupied by other geologists, but that early there was nobody around.

Shortly after arriving, Tony left to join the prospectors in the bush, and it was several weeks before we saw him again. So my mother-in-law and I filled our buckets from the hole in the ground, strained the water through muslin to get the weeds out, and heated them on the stove. This was our cooking, bathing, and laundry water.

We set to, and scrubbed the kitchen floor, and cleaned all the cupboards. Drove to Bathurst and bought packages and cans of food and settled in. Danny came to mend the broken steps and the screen door, and his two sons brought logs for the stove.

It wasn't very comfortable, and there was nowhere in town where we could rent furniture, so we just had to make the best of what we had. We kept the fire going, and the upstairs rooms were heated by a grill in the kitchen ceiling.

We had a small radio, and with luck we could get a classical music station from Boston hundreds of miles to the south, and in the evenings, we crouched close to the radio to hear it.

As the weather warmed, the bathroom upstairs began to leak and we placed our two big galvanized tubs underneath to catch the drips, and they plinked and plonked all day and night.

Those galvanized tubs were used for bathing and laundry too, of course no washing machine, but we had never had one anyway, so it was no hardship to do our laundry on a washboard using Sunlight soap, rinsing it in the other tub, and pegging it out on a line where it blew in the wind and came in smelling of sweet sea air.

By now the water had been turned on in the house and the leaks repaired, so life became a lot easier. It was truly fortunate that my mother-in-law (we called her Doe Doe) was there with me, and knew how to manipulate all the mysterious dampers and keep the fire going because this was used for cooking as well as heating. I'm sure I couldn't have stayed there on my own, nor would I have wanted to.

Amazingly we survived the way pioneers did by baking bread ourselves and as soon as we could, making a garden and planting salad greens, and tomatoes, carrots and onions, peas and beans.

The local people of Bathurst didn't seem to eat vegetables, or at any rate there weren't many in the stores in town. Some sad-looking cauliflowers, very elongated, all stalk and yellow at that, but we could get fiddleheads which were wonderful, like asparagus in a way. They were the unfurled fronds of a fern and looked exactly like fiddleheads. I've never come across them anywhere else.

But we noticed some greens growing in the next door fields and went to the farmhouse to see if we could come and pick some using the few French words we had and some sign language. They happened to be turnip greens, and starved for greens as we were they tasted wonderful. The farmer thought it was very funny that these strange English people would want to eat something they grew for the cattle.

And then as the snow melted, something miraculous happened. The mud flats turned green with growing water plants and sedges, and from the south across the Bay came the birds. We must have been on a migratory route, and the geese came first arrowing across in long shimmering lines, calling to each other.

Little birds I had never seen flew in and settled in flocks to rest and feed in the marshes, then they were replaced by others I cannot name, they came in droves. We were entranced and took Christopher down to the little wooden bridge to watch.

All spring the birds came by the hundreds on their way north. Later came grouse performing their strange mating dances right there in our field. And in the summer we watched osprey fishing in the sea. It was magical.

As the field grew into hay and the tractors came to cut it, so came the spiders into the house. One day in the shower, I counted fifty on the ceiling above me.

It was a very hot summer, Doe Doe and I sweltered with no air conditioning. We opened the windows, but in came hot air. Fortunately we were able to rent a refrigerator, and a small cooktop, so we didn't have to light the big iron stove which would have been unbearable, although I suppose the pioneers had to.

The geologists arrived to base in the house next door, mostly college professors researching geo-chemistry which was new at that time. Johnny Webb and John Tooms from the Royal School of Mines in London. Hal Bloom from the Colorado School of Mines in Golden, and Herb Hawkes from Boston, a lively crowd, like Tony though back and forth into the bush.

But the summer passed and they all went home, and once again we were on our own. Tony had been transferred to an area 100 miles north of Ottawa. He had been gone a month, and we knew that we should be leaving too, but the time dragged on and it was getting cold, very cold.

There was a telephone in the big house that had not been disconnected, and so every night I put on my parka and went across to telephone a bar in the town of Maniwaki where I knew the prospectors gathered sometimes. There was no other means of communication. It was October, I was 5 months pregnant and I daren't risk lifting trunks and driving to Ottawa without help. I needed desperately to reach him to come back to help us move before the snow came. Already the Northern Lights were spreading their drifting curtains across the sky, and the geese had flown south.

After about two weeks of nightly phoning, I got a welcome Scottish voice at the other end, it was one of our prospectors who happened to be in the bar. "Oh Davy" I said "Can

you get word to Tony that he has to come back"
and dear Davy Watson promised to do that." Is it
getting cold there Jeannie lass?" and I told him we
couldn't stay here much longer, this matchbox of
a house wasn't going to keep out the cold. I knew
I would have to drive us out soon regardless of
my pregnancy.

But Tony came, and we went to the train
station to meet him. What a welcome sight! The
steel trunks packed and ready were shipped to
Ottawa, and Danny's boys helped load the car.

Our journey to Ottawa took several days,
and the maple trees were ablaze with fall colors,
so wonderful, as though there was a light inside
each tree.

I had no regrets about leaving Bathurst,
and I have to admit that those seven months were
an unforgettable experience, but one I would not
want to repeat!

The End of An Era

It was October 1955 when we drove our blue Dodge out of New Brunswick in Eastern Canada, across Quebec into Ontario, and arrived in Ottawa at last. A long drive in a heavily laden old car, hoping it wouldn't break down and the tires would hold out!

I was five months pregnant, and the journey was hard on me, I was tense all the way. I had experienced two miscarriages before Christopher was born and was so anxious that I would be able to carry this baby full term, and get to where we could settle down and be quiet for a while.

Ottawa is a wonderful little city, the capital of Canada, it has the Parliament Buildings, and the Governor General lives in a large mansion in a beautiful part of town. There are some wonderful parks, and one in particular is filled with tulips in the spring, the bulbs sent over every year from the Netherlands as a thank you gift. Princess Juliana, later Queen of Holland was evacuated to Ottawa with her children for safety during World War II.

After a few days in a motel, we found a house to rent, where again the owners were going south for the winter, and we could move in immediately. What luxury after our meager living conditions in far away Bathurst. Comfortable rooms with real furniture and carpets on the floors. A kitchen with a proper stove and refrigerator, lots of hot water for showers, and oh, joy, a washing machine and a dryer. What bliss! You have to have lived without all these conveniences to really appreciate them.

Tony left almost immediately for the bush, so once more we were on our own. It became very cold, and the snow came early and stayed. I didn't think I should shovel the driveway, and so the car stayed in the garage, and we walked to the Supermarket with Chris in the sleigh. The store delivered for us, so it was no problem, and we used the streetcars whenever we went downtown.

Claire was born March 3rd, 1956 in a large Catholic Hospital staffed by nuns in long white habits. It was dark and gloomy and very dry, my throat hurt and I didn't feel well, but I was desperate to get home, so I didn't say anything. Unfortunately Tony had to leave, he'd already been home for a week, and so I had to go downstairs to the billing office and stand in line to pay, which I shouldn't have been allowed to do, and then get a taxi home with my baby.

The following month, April, we were moved back to Toronto. My mother-in-law, who had been with me for a year, returned to England, and we packed the car and took the long road back to Toronto, a full circle from when we left 18 months before.

Tony realized that with two children it was time to put down some roots, our nomadic days were over, and we needed a home of our own, so we found a motel on the outskirts of Toronto while we searched for a house.

To me, every house we looked at was marvelous, I went into ecstasies over each and every one, and so in the end, I was left behind in the motel with the children while Tony went on his own. This didn't please me very much, I wanted to be in on this very exciting experience of finding my first home.

But then one day Tony came back with the choice of two. A new subdivision was being built outside the little village of Agincourt on the very northern edge of Toronto. It was all countryside around, farms and fields, and now this little community of small homes.

There were two available, one just a regular suburban ranch-style house, the other had large windows and a sloping cathedral roof. Inside it was really just one large space with partitions. Up six stairs a gallery with three bedrooms and one bathroom leading off. Of course that was the house I chose, the price was $12,000, and the company lent us the down payment. We took out two mortgages on that little house and it was crippling, but it was our very first home, and we had to do it. The large backyard was just rough ground, still part of the field, it was built on. No trees, no grass. I was enchanted!

We had no furniture of course, being nomads all this time, so we stayed in the motel while we scoured the newspapers for estate sales. We bought two chairs and a couch from one place, a bed from another. We had to buy a refrigerator new, but a table and chairs had to wait, and we ate off our laps for some weeks. The house was equipped with a stove and unbelievably, a washing machine, I thought I was in heaven!
Everybody on the street was young like us, with babies or young children. Nobody had very much, and so we shared what we had. There was "the vacuum cleaner" and "the polisher" because in those days we waxed and polished our floors. There was also "the lawnmower", a push mower to mow the weeds that we all had in the beginning, there weren't power mowers in 1956. Then there was "the hat" and "the purse" for special occasions. Children's clothes were passed on to other children on the street.

A school was built nearby and the children all started school at Agincourt Elementary. In the spring they were taken to see the newborn lambs at the farm next door. The village was a walk away, and I put the baby in the carriage, and with Christopher on a little red tricycle, went down every day to the post office to get the mail from our box, and to buy groceries from the local IGA.

Three of our children were born from 12 Canham Cres., twice a neighbor had to drive me to the hospital because Tony was away. Once he was in Europe!

I made that rough ground behind the house into a beautiful garden, sowing grass seed, and digging into the clay anything I could find to loosen it, sand, peat moss, and even buckets of black earth from the swamp in the woods, but slowly, with cuttings begged from other friends' yards, flowers began to grow. Everybody in Canham Cres worked and made gardens where there had been nothing, it was a very happy neighborhood.

I still pegged my washing on the line because I loved to see it blowing in the wind and the diapers and sheets came in snowy white and smelling of fresh air. I would have a

91

clothesline now if it was allowed. In the winter of course it was a different situation when washing had to be pried off the line frozen solid, and blue jeans stood up on their own!

Back then we had snow from early November into May, and we never saw the ground all that time. We had a toboggan that was 6 feet long and we'd all pile on and slide down the snowy hills of Ontario. Tony was now home at weekends most of the time and we had some wonderful treks into the country tobogganing in the winter and picnicking in the summer.

Tony started his own company in 1961 the year Patrick was born and after a rocky beginning, things improved financially, and we even paid off the second mortgage!

However, with five children and two adults in a three bedroom house, and frequent visitors when we all had to squish up together, and just the one bathroom, it became obvious that we had grown out of 12 Canham Cres, and so very sadly we put the little house on the market. It sold very quickly with all the improvements we'd made and the trees we'd planted, for $14,000, and we moved to another subdivision not far away where the children each had their own bedroom and there were three bathrooms. I even had a dryer, but only used it in the winter. I still loved my clothesline.

Toronto was expanding in all directions. A big new airport for the jets that needed longer runways, immigrants pouring in, our lovely countryside disappearing as developers took over and built rows of boxes where the fields had been. All those century-old stone farmhouses swallowed up in new subdivisions, or simply demolished. I've got to admit that I shed a few tears over the loss of such treasures.

Our children grew, and Claire and Chris went to University and in 1976, Tony started another company in Denver, Colorado. With everything changing around us, and without really thinking it through, I said "Look, you can't start a company without being there, why don't we move to Denver?"

And so once again we put our house up for sale and applied for a Visa to the US, which was granted, and set a date to move.

Chris was then 24 years old and doing his Master's in Aerospace Engineering at University of Toronto, so he would stay behind and leaving him was one of the hardest things I ever had to do, but it was time.

Roger was taking his final exams at High School, so we got him a hotel room for a week, so that he could finish, and then he flew down when he was through. The rest of us saw our furniture loaded onto a big Mayflower van and followed it across the border. We left our beloved Canada after twenty-three years, and I for one left part of my heart there.

Our life of adventure didn't end at the age of fifty, it was the end of an era that's all, we simply opened a new door and went through into a different world.

Washing Day

I lifted the basket of laundry and put it on top of the dryer, then loaded the washing machine with light-colored clothes, sheets and towels, poured in the detergent, closed the lid and pressed the button.

I could have walked away, but this time I didn't. My mind drifted back in time to the late 40s and early 50s when Anthony and I were first married, living in London. We had 2 rooms at the top of an old 19th Century house, lots of stairs, and shared a kitchen and bathroom with another couple.

Washing day at that long ago time was a very different experience.

I remember putting laundry in the big kitchen sink, sprinkling soap flakes on top and pouring in the hot water. Then I went to work.

It was usually around 6:30 when I got home. The laundry a gooey mass sitting in congealed soap in cold water. I would let the water out, squeezing the clothes as the water drained away and pouring in more hot water.

My mind jumped back to the past while my washing machine swished and paused and then the tone changed as the washing water spun out and new clean water poured in.

In time gone by our supper was bought from the local fish and chip shop round the corner, so that we wouldn't have to use the sink for cooking.

So then I got out the washboard and Sunlight soap, and the evening was spent rubbing each item with soap and scrubbing it up and down the washboard, dropping everything piece by piece into a pail until my back ached. It remained to fill the sink with several rinse waters, and squeezing as much water as possible out. I think I have strong hands because of those times.

That old house had no backyard to hang clothes on a line, and so clothes, towels, sheets, everything was draped over a clothes horse with newspaper spread underneath and was left to dry, which often took a week in that cold house.

I stood for a moment remembering. Then slowly I put both hands on my now quiet washing machine, bent over and kissed it.

Football. Through the Eyes of a Brit

Six months after emigrating to Canada from Britain, we were traveling to our new assignment in New Brunswick from Toronto, via New York and Boston where we had friends.

Mistake No. 1!

It was Saturday when we arrived in Boston and called in on our friends. They were incredibly hospitable, welcoming us into their beautiful house, and insisting we stay with them for the weekend.

Mistake No. 2!

Allowing Herb, a fellow geologist to stay at home to talk with Anthony, and give up his cherished ticket to the football game between Yale and Harvard. And so it was that I went to my first and only football game.

Mistake No. 3!

We had absolutely no idea of the importance of sport to the American people.

In Britain there's soccer and cricket, but most people don't care who wins or loses. It's just a game after all, and divided more or less down class lines. The working classes go to soccer games on Saturday afternoons and the upper class support cricket, which as you might expect, stops for tea halfway through.

My experience of that football game was of sheer boredom. There were all these padded and helmeted gentlemen with a funny shaped ball pointed at both ends, crouched together in the middle of the field.

Somebody threw the ball and one man caught it, only to be pounced upon by somebody else, whereupon they all fell on top of him in a heap. The heaps occurred throughout the game they all seemed to enjoy falling and rolling about in heaps, but the ball didn't seem to go anywhere before there was another heap.

There were two goal posts but no net, and nobody seemed to get anywhere close to them, so as far as I could tell there were no goals scored.

I did ask my hostess at one time when they were going to score a goal, but she didn't give me a straight answer, she kind of choked.

I thought it was the most unbelievably slow game I had ever seen, but periodically everyone rose to their feet and cheered, so it was obvious that somebody had scored a goal, but I didn't see anything that resembled one, especially when there wasn't a net.

In the end I contented myself with looking at everyone in the audience. Americans looked so different from English people. They wore really nice clothes I thought, and made a lot of noise, and had they hair cut in funny ways.

I was glad when it was over and I could stand up. My hostess introduced me to a lot of people. Everyone seemed to know everyone else, and they all asked me "if I'd enjoyed the game, and wasn't I lucky to have been able to watch the game of the season between Yale and Harvard?" I said, "Yes" very politely, "I had enjoyed it immensely". My hostess choked again, and after what seemed like a very long time and shaking hands with a lot more enthusiastic people, we finally got into the car and went home.

I don't know who won, and didn't like to ask.

Later on, I realized what a sacrifice that must have been for our friend, and have been embarrassed about it ever since.

Now I make a point of never phoning anyone on Saturdays in case they should be spending the day watching sports.

This I do know, that the day of the world series or whatever it's called, is the very best day to go shopping at the Mall!

A Visit to Aunt Margie

I walked along the twisted lane that led to Aunt Margie's house. The washed air, sweet as growing grass, puddles reflecting the glinting sun as it came and went after the rain had passed.

The ancient stone walls green with moss and lichen hugged the fields.

Beyond the wooden five-bar gate the little tractor ploughed the field, turning the winter grass under, exposing the furrows of coal-black, beetle-black earth.

Seagulls swooped and dived, following the tractor, mewing and crying as they settled to eat, while it readied the soil for spring planting.

How I loved this narrow fertile strip of Moray close to the waters of the Moray Firth with the mountains of Ross and Cromarty beyond, sheltering it from the wild weather of the Northern Highlands.

Up past the little Loch of the Blairs I walked, skirting the glinting puddles, to the row of small granite cottages, "the wee hooses", where my Aunt Margie lived. The sweet smell of the smoke from a peat fire as it rose from the chimney.

Her "sit up and beg" bicycle, basket on the handlebars, leaned against the wall. Aunt Margie still rode her bicycle to town, even in her 80s. There was no telling her what she shouldn't do.

The old wooden gate creaked as I lifted the latch and walked through and I saw the lace curtain twitch as she heard my footsteps on the gravel path. The door swung open, and there she was, her white hair twisted into a knot on top of her head. A little woman, maybe 4'10", but bright as a silver button she was, smiling her welcome. "Come awa' ma bairn" she'd say, and I was swept inside and settled in a chair while she poked the fire into a blaze and put the kettle on to boil for tea.

She was gone for a moment and reappeared with a tray of freshly baked bannocks spread with butter and jam, and girdle scones.

We settled down to talk. She wanted to know all about my children, her great-nephews and nieces as we drank tea from bone china cups, and I wanted to know how her life was now that she had retired. My Aunt had been in service all her life, but there was not, nor had there ever been anything servile about her. She was smart and feisty, and full of energy and fun.

What a great little lady she was, and I miss her so much whenever I go to Scotland, but her spirit is always with me, following me around, telling me what I should or shouldn't be doing – not that I take any notice Aunt Margie!

The Army and Navy Club

"You have to stay there, it's central and cheap" our long and lanky English friend told us "if you like I'll propose you."

Well it being central was certainly attractive, and "central" meant Picadilly which was in the middle of London. "Cheap" was all the more attractive because no London Hotels are cheap.

My husband Tony made frequent business trips to London, and there were times when I went with him. Clubs like the Army and Navy were usually quite exclusive, I'd never been inside one but they sounded posh. I wasn't sure about that bit, we used B&B's whenever we were abroad, they are anything but posh and we liked it that way. But we were ready to give it a whirl.

So we were "proposed" and our membership card duly arrived. There didn't appear to be a fee, so maybe that was a good sign. It was possible that because Tony was a Ph.D. and had a Dr. in front of his name, he was considered the "right" sort of person.

If you know anything about the upper classes in Britain, you'll know exactly what I mean! We took a taxi to the Army and Navy Club and pulled up outside a Regency house of imposing size, iron railings in front and a gate, it was set back from the other modern buildings on either side, with a small garden and steps leading to a porticoed front door.

It certainly looked very grand and had obviously been a gracious London home at one time.

We opened the gate, mounted the steps, and rang the bell, there was no answer. Then we noticed a small discreet notice. "No Ladies are permitted to enter through the front door, with the exception of Her Majesty the Queen."

I was a bit taken aback by that, but we crept around the house to the side door where we were admitted by a dusty looking gentleman in a peaked cap and rumpled uniform jacket.

Inside there was a small dark lobby and an old fashioned cage elevator which propelled us to the 3rd floor. The dusty gentleman escorted us to our room which he opened with a long iron key.

The room contained a double bed with a shabby gold-colored coverlet, one overhead light, two night stands and a wardrobe with a flyblown mirror and a squeaky door. "Bathroom down the hall, clean the bathtub after you've finished" grunted the man, and off he went.

We sat on the bed and the springs twanged under us "but it was cheap" we kept reminding each other.

We decided to explore and went downstairs to the clubroom as it was called. Several retired admirals and generals sat around on brown leather chairs, either sleeping or behind newspapers. In unison the papers were lowered, and we came under critical scrutiny.

Not a word of greeting. I gave them a bright American smile "Good morning" I said, hoping for a response. The newspapers were all raised again.

We stayed one night on the twangy bed, and left as soon as we could, emerging with relief into the bustling, energized city of London, got on a big red double-decker bus and left the Army and Navy Club forever.

Letting Go

In 2009 I lost Anthony to Alzheimer's.

I feel I should write my story of Anthony's illness because it may help other people facing the same situation, not knowing what to expect. Anthony's story is not unique, other people's may be quite different. This is his.

It had been a long struggle, seven years since he had been diagnosed, and although he knew about his disease, he denied it vehemently. Each visit to the doctor he pronounced, "never felt better in my life, I feel as well as I did when I was twenty." My solution to this was to send the doctor a note ahead of time telling him exactly how things were with my husband, and what had happened during the past six months.

In truth though, for six and a half years, Anthony did remarkably well. He exercised, walked the trails behind our house twice a day with our dogs, although they escaped from him frequently because he simply forgot they were there, whereupon we had to wait for phone calls from sympathetic neighbors and I would drive up and rescue them.

At various times, I phoned the Alzheimer's Association, hoping to find out what to expect as his illness progressed, only to be told that I must get some help in the house in order to get a break. I knew this was true, but Anthony refused to accept strangers in the house, and the times I did find someone to come in, he promptly took off into the unknown. Then I would get a frantic call from the caregiver and I would have to return to search for him.

Many, many times I searched the dozens of small roads in our area, and I always found him just as long as he stuck to the roads and didn't wander off on the trails.

Once after a fruitless search I received a tip that he had been seen on the access road to the Morrison exit heading east towards Denver. I drove out of Genesee and down the hill almost to Golden, but realizing he couldn't have got that far without getting a lift, I turned around, stopping at the Conoco Station at the Morrison exit to get gas, and that's where I found him just heading home. He had walked seven miles at that point, and was obviously prepared to walk another seven miles home.

Another time, out with the dogs on the trail, he was gone about two and a half hours when I finally called the Genesee office for help. In ten minutes two police officers were at my door, a third arrived with a bloodhound soon after. I knew where he usually walked, but wasn't able to go myself because I was just home from the hospital with a hip replacement.

But the bloodhound got the scent from Anthony's pajamas and was able to trace him exactly where I told the police he went, but there was no sign of him. Shortly afterwards I got word from the office that a maintenance man had found him on the road, not lost, just taking his time and enjoying his walk. "Lovely day" he told the maintenance man.

They brought him home to find two police cars and a motorcycle on the driveway, and a very worried wife. I never did tell him about the bloodhound, he would have been mortified!

Stopping him driving was another matter. He swiped the side of another car while trying to find an unfamiliar street. He took the wrong ramp off the highway and got lost, and when finally I sat down to talk about it, he promptly left the room! In desperation I called the License Department, but they could do nothing unless he had an accident, the police said the same. In vain I begged them to remove his license before a terrible accident happened.

So one day while I was driving with him beside me, and couldn't get out and leave, I told him he was a danger to other people. "How would you feel" I said "if you killed someone, a child maybe, just think about it." He did, and finally agreed to let me do the driving. A rock on the road totalled his car and I managed to persuade him not to get another. "After all, we only need one car"!

During the last six months of his life, he followed me everywhere I went. I went down to the basement, he came down too. I went out to take the trash down, he was there behind me. He sat in the kitchen with me, he followed me up to my loft where I paint, and then he began to fall.

We would go for a short walk and he asked to turn around, he who only a year before had easily walked five miles. He never admitted that his legs had begun to weaken. One day he was with me in the garage while I was cleaning the extra refrigerator, when his legs crumpled and gave way. I called a neighbor for help, and between us we got him up and into the house.

By this time I was able to have help one day a week, a little Hispanic lady named Betty came in the morning and did the laundry, dried it, folded it and put it away. She also dusted the furniture, made coffee for Anthony and sat and talked to him. What a wonderful lady!

Thus I was able to go down the hill and paint with my friends. Anthony was quite happy with Betty in the house, and she would bring him down to meet me at a restaurant for lunch. It was a blessing to have her. I also had help from my daughter Elisabeth who gave me a whole morning and then took her Dad out for lunch in Evergreen, he loved that. My daughter-in-law Arlene came for a few hours each week and kept him company, or took him out. These three saved me.

Otherwise my days consisted of taking him for a short walk after breakfast, a drive to the grocery store where he would sit and drink coffee while I whizzed around with the cart, and this we did twice a week. I divided my grocery list in two so that I would have somewhere to take him. He never seemed to tire of going to the store where he could enjoy the flower display or watch the people.

Sometimes we'd go to the ice cream store where we would sit outside in the sun and watch the ducks in the creek and the children playing. Every day we'd go for lunch, always the same restaurant, always the same lunch "Eggs Benedict".

After lunch I'd take him home for a nap, then have a cup of tea, and go for a drive, a different one every day, but not too far. He would sit and enjoy the countryside, a slight smile on his face, perfectly happy to be driven.

His work and his Company seemed to be forgotten. He who for most of his life thought of nothing else, had received numerous awards and had been inducted into the Canadian Mining Hall of Fame. His brilliant mind had disappeared into a different world.

Instead of the driven man I had married, he became quiet and content with his life the way it had become. Grateful for the help he got from neighbors and family when they came to visit and take him out. Happy to be driven around the countryside, loving the sunshine and the blue Colorado sky, and the boxes and pots of flowers I planted on the deck.

I wish the Alzheimer's Association had been able to advise me as to what might happen. The following me around the house, the routines, the clinging, it was easier once I knew the patterns, but I had to forget my own pursuits, except for that one morning when Betty came and the hours when my daughters were able to squeeze out of their own full days.

I dreaded his falling in the night when I wouldn't be able to lift him. The falling was something else I had not anticipated. He who had been so strong and muscular, who walked ten miles so easily in the mountains when we hiked the trails.

Now he had become totally dependent on me, he wanted me there every minute of every day. So this was my life, a 36-hour day his doctor called it, and it was daunting, but true.

Then came the day when I had to have some minor surgery, and I asked him if he minded going to a senior assisted living for a week. I had made inquires at a local place, and they assured me they could take care of an Alzheimer's patient.

It was very nice there, meals were provided, and help showering and dressing if needed. In Anthony's case he could manage all that himself, but sadly, and astonishingly, his condition deteriorated so radically in that one week that he was not even able to get out of a chair without help and could only shuffle along. I was so shocked at the change in him, but his doctor told me he was on the brink of it anyway, and any change in routine would have triggered it. I realized I would not be able to look after him anymore.

A few days later I got a call from the Home to say they had discovered him on the floor cold and clammy when they checked at 7 am and had called an ambulance. He was at the hospital and I went immediately and found him in Emergency awaiting the doctor, which I may add took several hours. He was admitted, and kept overnight, but I was told he would not be able to go back to the Home, there was not enough care.

The family met me at the hospital, a decision had to be made, we needed to find somewhere quickly, and a Social Worker helped us find a Nursing Home, which was unbelievably depressing and gloomy. He sat slumped in a wheelchair and was so uncomfortable. I couldn't leave him there. And so began the search. My son and daughter-in-law visited four, and my daughter and I looked at four more, all equally depressing. We met in the evening exhausted and in despair.

And then I remembered Arlene, a nurse who had cared for a friend, was cheerful and capable, and who now looked after hospice patients, one at a time in her home.

I asked her whether she could take Anthony, begged her in fact, and she did, dear, dear Arlene. He was transferred by ambulance the next day and we followed and found him comfortably settled in a soft recliner covered with a light blanket. I knew he would be cared for there, and he was. Next day when I went, he had been wheeled outside onto the patio. There was a bird feeder full of birds, sitting beside him a large black elderly dog, and three cats. Anthony loved animals.

He died there after five days. All the family came to see him, and I went every day, and he knew us all. I telephoned his nephew in England, and Michael flew over to be with us, arriving just in time to say 'goodbye'. Anthony died in his sleep, very peacefully, he was 84. He had a long fulfilling life, accomplishing a great deal as a geophysicist. He called himself an "inventor", and that's what he was, forming two companies on his ideas alone, and wrote 40 patents. We have five children and four grandchildren. He was a very happy man.

In July of 2012, Chris, Julie and David were here from Canada on vacation, and Patrick flew in from Arizona. Our granddaughter Christine took the time to come from Minneapolis where she is at St. Olaf College, so amazingly, the whole family were here in Colorado at the same time.

We took Anthony's ashes to the mountains he loved, each of us carrying a small rock. We met close to Loveland Pass at a place where Anthony and I often went to sit quietly amongst the tussocky grass and the little mountain flowers. There we found a protected space beside a rock and spread his ashes. Each of us wrote a message and laid them under a small rock with a silver heart, given to me by a friend when he died, and then we built a cairn with our little rocks. It was the most peaceful and wonderful day, and Anthony is there in the mountains where he belongs.

I urge caregivers, hard as it may be, to find a nursing home you like, ahead of time because even though you may want to keep them at home, it may not be possible without help.

Realize that for however long it takes, your whole life will be devoted to caring for and loving this one person.

We were lucky that Anthony was happy with the care he had from all of us. He was never angry or violent and knew us all until the end.

The Geese

They called to me one morning
A strange rolling cry it was,
like tearing fabric
in the sky.
Then suddenly I saw a flock of geese
far far above.
I looked with longing
as they flew
like wreaths of smoke
pulling changing moving
ever Southward.
They called to me once more last night
I heard them crying
in the dark.
"Come with us" they seem to say.
It is as if I flew with them
once long ago
I too had strong and powerful wings
that beat upon the air.
Beloved geese God speed
go safely
and return next Spring
and take my heart
upon your wings

Summer Into Fall in Evergreen

I came into my little lavender-scented house a short while ago, welcomed by a symphony by Sibelius, my very favorite composer. I'm really a very Northern soul, and this music is redolent with the hills and forests of Finland, with rushing downhill streams into rivers to the sea.

I had been out hosing the garage in the late September sunshine, a crime to be inside on such a day, and I always leave the radio on to greet me with music when I come back in.

Outside, the trees are turning, shedding golden light everywhere, I feel so contented in this friendly place in Evergreen.

What a waste of six months in Littleton in that Senior Complex full of depressing people with canes, and walkers, and electric carts. Maybe I should have taken the time to get to know some of them, I might have found a few kindred spirits.

I stuck it out for six months, feeling dragged down by the proximity of these old people who didn't have the energy I have. I knew I had to get out of that place, and my friend and realtor said one day after we'd looked at the umpteenth small house in Littleton "You're never going to be happy down here, why don't you go back to the mountains where you belong?"

So many times last summer, I would come back up here and walk, or sit by the lake and cry, or drive to the mountains by Georgetown, over Loveland Pass, and down into Keystone and Dillon, and feel the pull of the High Country.

So I followed my heart and moved, the second move in a year which is crazy I know, but what a welcome I got from all my friends here, hugs wherever I went.

It has been worth all the stress.

The Motto? Follow Your Heart!

The Woman Who Walks by Herself

I am the meadow
in the park
where the woman
walks by herself
every day.

She is a little slower
nowadays
than she used to be
and walks carefully
when my path is icy.

Sometimes I see
her pause
and put her hand
upon my tree to rest
and catch her breath

And then I send
my warmth and energy
into her hand
from my tree's trunk
and on she goes.

But as the sun gains strength
my baby roots reach down
into the wet earth
and I push the green shoots
up to greet the sun.

I see the woman
who walks by herself
stand in awe and delight
as the grass begins
to grow and spread.

The woman
stops more often now
looking at the greening
of the land
and breathing the warm spring air.

She holds
the rough bark of my tree
as if to bless
the rising sap
the tree's blood.
I notice that
she bends to pat
and talk to every dog
that passes
with a touch of sadness.
So with the spring
my grass grows
tall and lush
and moves and dances
in the wind.
The woman who walks by herself
sees each new flower
as it blooms.
Every day a new one
amongst the waving grass
And so I give the gift
of joy and delight
to the woman
who walks by herself
in the park every day.

The Wind Am I

Have you smelled the sweet soft rain
    Coming in across the hills?
Have you smelled the stormy, salted sea
    borne inland,
            squalling, squalling?
I am wind, the wind am I.

Do you hear the singing through the cracks,
    the sighing in the night?
Do you hear the cracking trees,
    the struggling branches,
        calling, calling?
I am wind, the wind am I.

Did you see the ripples on the lake?
    The push and pull of waves amongst the
grass?
Did you see the bending, stretching trees?
    The flying snow,
        falling, falling?
I am wind, the wind am I.

Forecast Snow

Grey skies glowering,
　　　　Cold wind from the West
　　　　　　　bringing snow.
Settling on the cold earth
　　　　covering
　　　　　　　last year's yellow grass.

Brown doggie eyes
　　　　under lifted brows
　　　　　　　entreating.
In vain
　　　the explanations.
Finally,
　　　padding myself
　　　　　　with extra trousers
sweater and coat,
　　　scarf, gloves and hat,
I take the leash
　　　and snap it into place.
Out in the punishing wind we go
　　　　Head bent against the snow,
　　　　　　　stumbling, sliding.

I let her go,
　　　she's off.
Burrowing, rolling in ecstasy,
　　　leaping high.
　　　　　　her paws on springs
The snow stings my cheeks,
　　　I shiver
as the cold finds my body.
　　　I watch in awe
　　　　　　this bounding energy.
This joy personified.

108

Rock

I walk

through the deep spruce laden forest,

Step over your rippling roots

that threaten to trip me.

Smell your sweet heavy pine scent,

touch your grooved bark,

uncover the orange skin beneath,

Feel the energy within you.

I climb

out of the forest and into aspen woods

shivering gently in the summer breeze.

Silvery green is your trunk

scarred by elk,

bent by ice storms long ago,

lifting your head towards the sun.

I wrap my arms

around your smooth body

and lay my face upon you.

Where is your spirit aspen?

I come at last

into the high meadow

shimmering with wild flowers.

There is a rock

resting ankle high

black it is, banded with quartz.

I move it gently, turn it with my foot,

push it from the earth

Wherein it lies.

Turn it, kneel then,

hold it in my hand.

The answer

Long, long have I lain here.

Cold and damp

Within the earth.

Now I can feel the sun

See the light for the very first time.

Feel your hand touch my face,

Sense the life within me.

The next snow

will roll me gently

down the hill and into the river below.

There I will rest until Spring,

the river will wash me clean

and take me down, down

to the lake in the valley beneath.

Then my wild spirit

will be freed at last into the sun,

released from the darkness

that was under the earth

for so long.

The Journey

The road stretches and ribbons

toward the west.

Elbows past small towns,

bent and cornered cliffs,

ancient and contorted.

Bypasses ox-bow tracks,

loops of an older highway.

Rocks, like houses, straddling.

Climbing now, paper-clip curves.

Forests hugging slopes,

waving, beckoning.

Ever higher, twisting

past banks of sliced snow.

Distorted trees,

leafless, stunted, clinging.

I am the road

that crests the last horizon

and clasps within my hands

the mountain sky.

Rock Spirit

Rock in my hand
grey, torn with green
threaded with quartz.

lifted from the earth
where you lay
imprisoned so long.

Do you feel the sun, rock?
Is the spirit within you
yearning to be free?

You are round and smooth
were you once a river rock
tumbled in the moving water?

Were you born on a mountain?
Did the ice of ages shatter you?
The storms of long ago

wash you down
into the seething river
roll and smooth you

then bury you
in the drying land
where I find you now.

I must leave you here
beside the mountain stream
where your spirit is free

to rise and dance
in the pure mountain air
once more.

Treasured Land

There it stands, built of stone
"raked from the fields" they said
"by a Scottish settler as he cleared his land."
Even now, with hollowed windows,
broken door, the steps remain
lilacs planted then on either side
"for luck" they said,
a row of pines, shielding the house
from wind and snow still stand.

This house has seen so much.
A mother cradling her new born child
the father carrying a tiny lamb
through the snow for shelter in the house.
The children swinging in the apple trees
bridal-white with blossom in the spring.
The yeasty smell of baking bread
Scottish bread high and dark.
The farmhouse, warm from the boot black stove
always the cauldron of soup simmering there.

The barn weathered and leaning now
strong timbers still support the roof
angled as a cathedral, beautiful to see.
Then though, warm with brindled cows,
strong and sturdy Clydesdales
stamped and snorted for their hay,
steaming horse-smells filled the barn,
harness and bright brasses hung
ready for the ploughing next day.

Here the fields are, furrows filled with clover
empty now. No cows or horses linger here.
All gone, long gone.
No happy voices fill the house
Empty now, empty.
No washing blowing in the wind.
No chickens peck for corn around the door.
All gone, long gone.
The sign beside the road reads
"Land for Sale" and "New Development"
My throat aches with sadness
as I watch the big machines
smash through this treasured land
cleared with love so long ago
by my Great-Grandfather.
All gone now, all gone.

Jazz

The exhileration
of four old musicians
oblivious to everything
but their music.
Joy emanating,
rolling in waves
like a Bach Fugue.
The rhythmic pounding
of fingers flying over
keys and strings,
flinging phrases
one to another
and dancing through
the vibrating air.

Tree Song

I stand tall in the forest,
my branches wave gently
in the spring breeze,
buds, red now,
Swelling with unborn leaves.
Warmed by the sun
my sap-blood rises
and pushes into life
my leaf-babes.

"Unfurl now children,
shine with yellow-green,
reflect the sun,
bring me your tiny flowers,
call the bees to kiss you."

Soon the flowers will fade
but now I feel within me
the fruit that is the meaning
of it all.

Through the summer
the fruit will swell,
my bark will crack
as new skin forms.

Fall comes slowly
but my seed
released from stalks
will fall into the fertile ground
around my roots.

Cool winds loosen leaves
now golden brown with age.
"You must fall too my children,
but your lives are not complete.
Now you must cover my seeds
and nourish the ground."

"Next Spring life begins again
and I must hold you close
protecting all I have nurtured
through the years."

117

Studio

This space is mine alone.
White walls embrace me
books sidle close together
on a shelf.

Paintings large and small
framed and unframed
pinned to the wall.
Empty frames ready and waiting
to be filled.

Large white table
loaded with the accoutrements
of my creativity.
Tubes of paint
butcher tray palette
jar of brushes
Paper stapled to a board
ready to go.

I cannot wait,
I lift my biggest brush
and throw the color
onto my clean empty paper.
Orange and red blend
and flames,
blue turns the red purple.

My heart pounds
with excitement
as the colors spread
and then I pull it all together
with black ink
which feathers into the damp colors,
and a form
begins to emerge
free and loose and wonderful.

This room liberates me
No walls enclose me here.
No one to strangle
the ideas that are mine alone.

All that I want to do
I can.

The Retreat

"Look", they said, "see the beauty of this tranquil place,
Hear the silence - we are all at peace with one another,
Nothing jars - no conflicts, only the merging of our souls.
Our love for all mankind".

"What do you do" say I, "how do you fill your time?"
"We think, we talk, discuss the outside world, we meditate,
we pray. We see the sky, the earth, the rocks, and
know that God is here.
It is enough - and all should have such peace."

I looked, and saw the clear tranquility
The smooth white, bright unruffled purity.
And sure enough no harshness,
No jangled clamour there.
No frenzied frantic voices, nothing loud.
Only the gentle sound of soft simplicity.

I am not wise like these contented souls.
I do not know this passive God,
Such peace is like a blanket covering.

Maybe for an hour, or even two
to contemplate the sky, the earth, the rocks.
Then I must be up and walking
Painting the shapes I see.
Searching for words to wind around the thoughts,
creating poetry,
Looking for myself.

There are no vibrant reds and pinks
to shimmer shine and glow,
Only the soft grey silver shadows
Pulling - smothering.
The God these people love
Is introspective - quiet.
It is the inner peace that lies within each one of them.

But no ideas flow,
No flowers or vegetables will grow
While hands lie empty.
No fires burn to spark creativity
Which is the meaning of it all.
No challenge to bounce against the walls of one another.
Excitement there is none.
No music is composed in this transcendent place.
The utter joy of dance and song does not exist
in this enchanted space.
Only the quiet - the other worldly calm,
The energy that is the point of life
Is gone.

Carolyn's Class

They sit,
      this circle of ordinary women
from a multitude of backgrounds.
      All with memories
          striving to be free.

They write,
      haltingly at first,
hesitating to bare their souls
      to strangers.

Yet one by one,
      amazingly,
like windblown butterflies
      the words appear.
Beautiful, emotional,
      deep with feelings
long buried within
      these extraordinary women.

A richness undiscovered
      until now ..
A new world
      that is bright and free
and theirs alone
      to explore
         and cherish.

The River

Mountain leaf, heavy with rain,
droplets gather,
plummeting into the waiting earth.
One by one, faster, faster,
until the trickle
becomes a single stream.
Sun picked water, sparkling,
channelled by crevices.
Down, down,
through tunnels of leaves.
Gathering speed, flying spume,
high in the air.
Down into pools of darkness,
pierced by sun.
Out of the rockland,
round, round,
corners and banks of silver sand.
I become a river.

Moving On

This house has been our home
for thirty years
and soon it will be time
for us to leave.

Eight other times we left a home
I put my soul each time
in yet another space
To start with two small rooms
on the top floor
of a big old house
in London
and lucky we were
to find those.

Fifty stairs, I counted them
up to where we
put our roots
for the first time.
We were married there
our furniture was old
passed on by
sympathetic friends.

Each time we moved away
I wept
and carefully unwrapped
the shroud of love
and wove another.

The Rains Came

The rains came
this Summer,
slanting from
an angry sky,
pounding
the bare earth,
overflowing
gutters,
dancing
through puddles,
flowing along
rivered roads,
down into
culverts,
and so into
the grateful lake,
and all is
suddenly quiet
once more.

The Quilts

I created something from my heart,
    An emotion that reflected
        my innermost thoughts.
I wove three quilts
    that gave me
        the utmost joy.
Full of colours that moved and shone,
    and danced and sang,
        and I hung my soul for all to see and share.
Some gave them not a glance.
    Some let their eyes drift over,
        with never a spark to respond
            to the fires that created them.
"Lovely" they said, and passed on.
    But others, just a few,
        were drawn as if by magnets
        to my dancing quilts.
The colours made music for them too.

Seen in Starbucks, King Soopers

Pre-teen girls standing in groups
eyeing the boys
self-consciously flipping
long shining hair.
Giggling at nothing.
Smart phones in every hand.
Short shorts
much too short,
threadbare jeans
holey knees,
flip-flops
painted toenails.
Conversation
full of "like"
and "you know."
A lot of growing up
to do, but oh
how lovely to be young.

River Rock

I am a rock, large, rugged
striped with white quartz
when rocks were molten
long before memories.

Out of the dark sky
came the rains
seeping through
the white quartz.

From the hot clear sky
the sun pierced my fissures
and I broke apart
where the white quartz veined.

Frozen by the cold winter ice
torn apart and smashed
by earthquakes
into a thousand pieces.

Now I am one of those
pieces of rock.
Washed down by rains
into the river below.

Rolled by the tumbling water
into a small
smooth stone
with a white quartz eye.

Seeing the sun
as it pierces
the cool clear water
where I lie.

Feeling the gentle
stroke of trout
pushing me onto
a smooth warm sand-bar.

There I can see
the large rugged rocks
from whence I came,
knowing that they too
will weather and break apart
roll down to the river
and become small smooth
stones
with white quartz eyes.

Wind

Winter clings on.
Brief snow flurries
spot the path like tears
melting as they breathe,
the warm air rising.
Icy wind
shouts its last defiant cry
screams through bare branches
already red
with new sap
rising like a blush
staining a young girl's cheeks.
Clatttering down roads
on garbage day
rolling the cans
down the hill
hiding lids.
Tossing plastic bags
high in the air
like kites.
Lifting hawks
soaring and tumbling
out of control.
But after all,
this March madness ends
as a balloon deflates
with a snort.
The winter wind
waves his gusty hand
"I'll be back," he laughs
"You can be sure
I'll be back."

Returning

Out of the mist
barely visible,
the swans return
like silent ghosts
from the North.
Long necks pulsating
up and down
heaving their bodies
towards the warm springs.
Symbols of rebirth
bringing new life
back to the island.
Powerful wings
white as the mist
surrounding them,
flap softly
as sheets on a line,
feet pressed forward
and come to rest
breaking the warm waters
of their remembered
homeland.

Disillusionment

It was Spring Break
and I took my 13-year-old granddaughter
with her friend, out for the day.
Lining the roads were ice-cream trees
vanilla, and strawberry.
"Look" I said "how beautiful they are"
"Mm" they said, cell phones in their hands.

We drove along the Foothills
"Did you know" I said "that long ago
great seas lapped against these hills?"
That three-toed dinosaurs
left their foot-prints in the mud
beside these hills?"
"Mm" they said, cell phones in their hands.

I took them down the road
to the Railroad Museum.
"See" I said "these great engines
pulled the trains from Eastern States.
People came to settle,
men came to mine in Central City.
What was the railroad then,
is now a highway.
"Mm" they said, cell phones in their hands.

"Did you know" I said "that Golden was the Capital
and a supply camp for the mines?
All the streets were thick with mud,
ladies trailed their long skirts in the mud.
What do you think of that?"
"Mm" they said, cell phones in their hands.

I drove them back to Littleton
dropped them off at home.
"Thanks" they said, and slammed the doors.
Cell phones in their hands.

Return to Como

In June of 1977, as recent arrivals in Colorado, we took the family and set out to explore and discover our new State.

Every weekend we would pack a lunch, study the map and then decide where to go. One of our first excursions was along Highway 285 to Fairplay. We stopped at every historical marker, tracing the history back and finally topped the rise of Kenosha Pass.

There lay the vast expanse of South Park, the green grass shimmering in the hot July sun. "Most probably a large lake originally" my geologist husband told us, "left by the glaciers as they retreated, leaving mounds of sediment, called drumlins, along the way." A lesson in geology brought South Park to life, I have loved it ever since.

Slowly we made our way along the valley, looking for a picnic table but finding none, we turned right onto a little dirt road to Como.

It was a shadow of a town that prospered long ago. A few abandoned, boarded up houses, others collapsed, the remains of a roundhouse that told us this had been a railroad junction and off on a dirt track we stopped by the cemetery.

There was an uneven wrought iron fence around it and a rusty gate. Inside it was overgrown with aspen and long grass, untended for many years.

We opened the rusty gate, creaking on its hinges and pushed aside the grass to find the graves. Totally hidden were pitiful little markers to "Our Baby" and then one by one the families. A lot of families died here, all buried together in clusters. Why? What happened to them?

Close by, leading through a forest of aspen trees, the remnants of the railroad leading towards the mountains, we found old railroad ties and cinders.

This sad little town lay forgotten in South Park and we wanted to know more about it, so we went to the museum in Fairplay. There they told us how very cold it is in the winters. Fires stacked high with wood could have burned the homes to the ground, the families with them.

Illnesses like measles, influenza and diphtheria took a lot of children. No doctor in town, deep snow prevented one coming from Fairplay and no telephones to summon one anyway.

It all haunted me and has done so to this day.

Recently, my daughter and I decided to go back to Como almost forty years later. Turning onto the same little road we found to our surprise the roundhouse restored. A large plaque recounted the history of this town. Coal mining had brought trains from Colorado Springs, Leadville and Buena Vista and across Boreas Pass from Breckenridge. Como became a hub.

The houses are being restored and lived in, there is a small hotel and gift shop, new homes are being built, everything painted and fresh.

Elisabeth and I retraced our steps to the cemetery only to find it too has been restored and reclaimed from the wild. The fence is new, the aspens removed, the grass cut, there is even a bench.

We found the gravestones cleaned and cared for. It didn't seem so sad after all. I went through the gate to stand for a time to look at South Park lying there, the October grass shining gold in the low sun of fall, the dark green pines beyond and the sweet dry scent of hay recently cut.

I felt happy we had returned to find somebody else had cared enough about Como to bring it back to life.

The Road to Creede

It was the last part of our week-long trip.

My daughter Elisabeth had organized and planned it, knowing I needed a vacation very badly. She also did all the driving, no small feat.

From Lake City, Colorado, we drove to Creede, and as we topped the high ridge, the whole valley opened up before us. Wide and green speckled with little hillocks left behind by an ancient glacier, called drumlins I learned.

Lined on both sides by mountains, the clouds drifted, casting their moving shadows, like giant mobiles over the entire valley.

Scarred in places by boulders dropped by the glaciers, the sparkling river wound down the middle, bordered with sedges turned red by the dipping sun, the green of the grass was suddenly gold, and the folded valley became Creede.

Life Dust

Up there, way up high, where no trees grow,
    there are mountain flowers.
So small, so small, you have to kneel
    in the sparse mountain grass
to see them.
        Always yellow though, or blue.
          Why is this?

I think it must be because the bees
    are attracted to these colors.
The yellow and blue flowers
    tiny as they are
must propagate to live.

So the bees flock to the breasts of them,
    gather the golden pollen
and scatter it into a cloud of life dust.

Trail Revisited

Trailhead reached
over rocks and ditches
risking broken axles
and flat tires
to get there
but still we did it.

Shouldering packs following trails
through pines and aspens
crossing the river
in full spate
treading the log
that spans it.

The trail winds up through meadows
filled with mountain flowers,
crossing creeks barefoot
up to where
the trees grow smaller,
up to where
the crystal lake
lies shimmering
in the alpine sun.
Icy cold to touch,
the air like wine
around us.

There, high in the mountains
the whole world
spread before us.

I will never forget
those hiking days
and even then
we were not young.
It's as though
we knew the days were short,
that our time
to climb these hills
would end.

But the memories
of those precious days
will live forever.

Spring Planting

The morning came
brimming with Spring,
We waited no longer
Sharon and I
Down the hill to O'Tooles
we went.
Wandering the aisles
breathing deeply
the scent of growing flowers
massed in singing colors
waiting for the happy gardeners
like Sharon and me.
Loading our carts
"Let's try these!"
Thinking of nothing
but planting our space.
Filling our shared garden
picking up boxes
of smiling plants
and smiling back,
Sharon and I.
Knowing that back-breaking
hours lay ahead.
Amending the beds
with rich compost soil.
Digging, watering, planting
our precious boxes
of instant joy
with love and hope
Sharon and I.

Coldwater Creek

In Two Thousand Ten it was,
my sister came to visit.
A long, long way it was
across the pond
to Denver.

I gathered her together,
tucked her in the car,
drove home quietly,
put her to bed,
and woke her
in the morning.
We walked and talked
endlessly it seemed,
and then we went shopping
to Coldwater Creek.

We went to Cherry Creek,
as well
as Park Meadows, we did,
then back to Coldwater Creek
where the Sales were on.
A better Sale every day
it seemed,
so of course
we had to go again
to Coldwater Creek,
to see what other bargains
could be found.

Time after time we went,
Seven trips in all, we took.
Each day
better than the last.
I sat there
watching her delight
as she gathered
a whole new wardrobe
loving every moment
of her day.

A blue jacket,
tops of all colors,
scarves,
stylish blouses,
simple tees,
a red parka
she has worn now
two seasons
in a row.

The ladies at Coldwater Creek
welcomed my sister
when she came.
Rushed around they did,
finding new things
for her to try.
She was a willing victim
so she was.
Bags of loot
came home from
Coldwater Creek
and piled up on the floor
they did.

Then when time came
to go back
to Scotland,
she left behind
all she had brought
across the pond,
and filled her bags instead
with Coldwater Creek.

The Symphony

How can this be?

    A collection of notes

set together in a pattern

    yet it can cause indescribable sadness

soaring elation,

    infinite joy.

Dimly aware of the audience around us

    but drawn together

    by silver threads of emotion.

The breathless anticipation

    and the echoing of a single instrument

as the music bursts like a Spring tide

    upon a sandy shore

    sweeping all before it.

The Bird in Winter

I perch on the rail
in the cold
and the snow that fell
last night
covers the seed
they put out for me.

I know how to keep warm,
my mother taught me
to fluff out my feathers
so that I am
like a little ball of fluff.

There is a flower pot
down there
I will fly to the bird feeder
and get some
sunflower seeds
then fly to the flower pot
to eat.
It is a haven,
a place out of the wind
They put some sphagnum there
maybe that was
for me.
I will come back
to this house
where they warm
the water
in the bird bath
and fill the feeder
with sunflower seeds
for birds like me.

The Cinderella Ball Dress

Grandma's Voice

It was Christine's and Sarah's day at Grandma's house. We went downstairs, Kelty and I, to fetch the white plastic boxes of toys. Kelty loved it when the children came, she wagged her tail and danced on her big paws, she was a mother dog even though she never had babies of her own.

We put the boxes on the living room floor and went to make cookies, Kelty and I. She sat on the kitchen floor waiting for bits of dough to drop. She knew there would be a cookie for her when they were baked.

Christine's Voice

The doorbell rang and Grandma came to open it giving Sarah and me a big hug. Kelty was there too with her big furry tail wagging. Kelty is as big as I am and bigger than Sarah who is only three. I am Christine and I am five. I can smell cookies baking. There are always cookies baking when we go to visit Grandma, oatmealie ones with raisins in them.

Sarah and I run to open the toy boxes and forget about Mommy and Daddy. In the boxes are wooden railroad tracks and little trains. There are bridges and tunnels and a station with little wooden people.

I can put the tracks together. Sarah can't, she's too little, but I make them go all over the room; under the table and the sofa, and the trains run over the bridges and through the tunnels and stop at the station to pick up the people to take them to town.

Kelty likes the trains too, sometimes she walks all over them and sits on the tracks and I get mad and shout at her. Kelty gets sad then and goes behind the chair and puts her head down between her paws. And then I feel sorry about Kelty being sad, so I go and stroke her warm head and I say "It's alright Kelty, I can put it back together" and Kelty licks my face.

The best time though at Grandma's house is when we all sit in the big arm-chair and eat a warm cookie and Grandma reads to us. I like Cinderella best because she has a fairy godmother who waves her wand and changes the pumpkin into a coach so Cinderella can go to the ball. Then she changes Cinderella's kitchen clothes into beautiful ball dresses. I like the pink one the best.

Grandma says she will make me a pink Cinderella dress, I am really excited about that.

Grandma's Voice

So I went to the fabric store to see what I could find. I didn't have a pattern but I thought if I bought a pink leotard and sewed a skirt on it, it would look kind-of-like a ball dress. I bought pink taffeta lining and a lot of pink tulle not realizing what I had let myself in for. I set the machine on the long gathering stitch and started on the tulle. But the tulle had a mind of its own and in no time it floated in a frothy cloud over my head obscuring my vision, but I persevered. It took me a very long time to make that skirt.

I gathered it onto a ribbon to tie around Christine's waist and sewed sequins on the leotard neck and sleeves. I was quite proud of it when it was finished. It didn't look exactly like the picture in the book but I hoped Christine wouldn't mind too much. I wrapped it in pink tissue paper and put it into a dress box for Christmas.

Christine's Voice

When it was Christmas we went to Grandma's house for supper and presents. Grandma hid the presents so we had to find them. Of course, I had to help Sarah find presents because I am bigger than she is. We carried each one down to the living room and put them on the table and on the floor. There were a lot of presents. Everybody had presents and there was Christmas paper all over the floor. Kelty hid under the paper and tore it into pieces with her teeth.

There was a big present for me and I didn't know what it could be, but then I took the lid off. There was tissue paper and inside the most beautiful Cinderella ball dress. Grandma helped me put it on and I really did look like Cinderella.

I ran to show everyone and twirled in it and danced and everyone clapped. It was the most wonderful Christmas ever; I will never forget my Cinderella ball dress.

Love from Christine

142

The Misadventures of Jean Barringer

Conventions are not my "cup of tea", I'd better tell you from the beginning, neither are luncheons, formal dinners, or cocktail parties. I never see the point of standing around with a glass in my hand talking about nothing, especially when I don't drink anything but tea. So I would have water and retire to a dark corner and wait it out.

This convention was to be in New Orleans and since I'd never been there, I thought I'd go. I was expected to go apparently, since my husband was vice president of the SEG (Society of Exploration Geophysicists) and Anthony was a geophysicist.

We flew to New Orleans and took a taxi to our hotel where the convention was being held. In the morning, I went down to the River Walk and there beside the dock was a paddlesteamer about to leave for a sail down the Mississippi. "Wonderful" I thought and got on. I'd never seen the Mississippi before and there was a running commentary of the history and stories and songs. The tour lasted about two hours and I sat in the sun and lapped it all up.

In the afternoon I wandered down to Bourbon Street absorbing this wonderful bric-a-brac place and returning to the hotel I signed up for a bus tour of Plantation Houses the next day.

I came down to earth in the evening when we went to the President's Dinner, to be confronted by the ladies, stuccoed and perfumed wearing glued-on smiles and fancy dresses. I don't remember what I wore, certainly nothing fancy. "Mrs. Barringer where were you? We expected you to join us on the excursion we had planned and tea, but you were nowhere to be found?"

I explained how I had been on a paddle steamer and how I had enjoyed it so much and I didn't know anything about your plans, how could I?

Apparently a program had been sent to us which thankfully I hadn't read and knew nothing about. It's entirely possible Anthony forgot to give it to me. Maybe even he didn't read it!

"Well of course Mrs. Barringer, you'll be joining us tomorrow for another very special tour won't you? We are meeting in the lobby at 9:30 and also, don't forget the dinner on the river boat at 5:00."

Oh my God, now what do I do? I didn't want to cancel my tour and didn't intend to either, so I came right out and looked at the "committee ladies" faces and told them. "Thank you but I've already made plans of my own for a bus tour of the Plantation Houses that I am really anxious to see."

Somehow I don't think people knew quite what to make of the contrary English woman who wasn't going to fall in with their plans!

Off I went the next morning and it was something I will never forget. The bus driver knew his history. He passed around books, explained why the houses were built the way they were with porches all round and windows for cross-draughts, it was all so interesting and we explored three or four of these spectacular houses.

The bus arrived back at the hotel late that afternoon and getting out of the elevator who should I meet on their way down but the dinner group! What could I say but "Oh Hi" and rush past them.

Needless to say Anthony was furious, all dressed and ready to go waiting for me and there I was, late and not at all ready. Suddenly it all hit me as incredibly funny and I began to laugh and then so did he.

We finished up going for dinner at a nice little restaurant on the River Walk overlooking the river, when unbelievably who should sail by but the convention group on their river boat. With one accord we both dived under the table helpless with laughter just as the waiter came to take our order.

How my poor husband explained his wife's erratic behavior I'll never know and if I was never invited to an SEG Convention again I would completely understand and it wouldn't worry me one little bit.

David's Music

I watched the boy
who was David.
I saw him grow
and respond to music.
To Beethoven, and Bach
even before he learned
to play them.
But he only played notes
from the printed page,
so I told him
"Music has to come
from your very soul"
and I knew right then
that David had to travel
along a different path.

Then at High School
David found Jazz,
and suddenly
he was transformed.
His fingers knew
what his soul
had been telling him
all along.
They came across the keys
in rhythmic patterns,
transposing one key
to another.
His fingers knew where to go
and the joy of the music
was David's.

Waterfall

Edge of rock - water falls
>   Down down, over and down.
Droplets caught by sun,
>   turned to spray, down, down.
Sheeted water hurled below,
>   Canyoned, channelled, pulled apart,
>   thrust once more into
>>   a common stream.
Mist rising to the edge of rock.

A Winter Walk With Ben

Encumbered as I am by coat and scarf

    Hat and gloves, long-johns, pants

      and gaitered boots,

I stumble, slide, and slither through the snow,

    Step on the crust, and immediately go through.

While Ben, his golden fur alight with sun,

    Leaps free, and bounds,

      His paws on springs,

His frosted whiskered face

    afresh from burrowing.

The air around him bright with diamonds.

I curse and swear, the cold strikes deep within me,

    While Ben is joy personified.

A Letter From My Mother

Dear Jeannie,

At this late stage in my long life
I need to tell you this.
You have closed the door on me
and I need you to open it
and to please understand me.

Growing up second eldest of fourteen
was not easy, you must understand this.
I had no time, or chance to be a child
I had to be a mother
to each new baby as it came.
Do you understand?

My Mom and Dad were strict, they had to be,
to keep us all in line.
My mother used a cane on our bare legs
My father, a strap on the boys.
They worked hard to feed us
There was very little money
but we grew up strong and tough.

I had no education.
The teachers gave me sewing to do.
I was good at it, but I learned nothing
in class, no reading or writing at all.

Each time a new baby came along
I stayed at home to help;
sewed beautiful clothes for the babies
dressed them, showed them off
and disciplined them
with my hand on their bare skin.

When you were born Jeannie
I had a chance again.
I dressed you up, and combed your bright curls
and showed you off, you were my doll.

I didn't know of course
that you were not a doll.
You were a child with a very strong will,
you stood up to me, you did
but I wouldn't have it.

I smacked you down
with my wet hand on your bare skin.
I didn't know there was any other way.

You asked me once when you were very young
what it felt like to be in love.
I told you there was no such thing as love
and remember the look of shock
upon your face.

You see, I didn't know about love.
I had never experienced such a thing
even from my parents you understand.
Nobody hugged me or said 'I love you'
never told me how beautiful I was
and so, I never gave you any love
I simply didn't know how,
and sadly Jeannie, I still don't.

                                    Mother

Moment Poems

1) Flying in over jigsaw fields
as the sun rises
over England.
Green, green, stitched
by hedgerows
One bright yellow field
of mustard
lights my tired eyes.

2) Dusty road
winds through folded hills
Brief stop
in sun-baked village
of Southern Spain.
Patch of sunlight
two little girls
dance a Sevilliana.

3) Oasis of green
midst the dusty hills
of Andalusia
group of washer girls,
laundry baskets
balanced on ink-black heads
taking a break
dancing a Sevilliana
Nightingale sings
in a tree overhead.

4) So much depends upon
being able to see
tone against tone
light against dark.

Consignment

At the end of the season I vowed, I would gather together the clothes I hadn't worn for two or three years, or more, and take them to the Consignment Store or Goodwill.

Every year I told myself this, for years and years in fact, but could never bring myself to part with the fragments of my life that had held such special memories for me.

The beautiful black evening dress with the black velvet scoop-necked bodice, empire waist, and long sleeves, and the charcoal silk sweeping skirt that swung around my ankles when I danced with my husband of fifty years, the dress I wore for our anniversary party.

I must tell you, that that anniversary party was twelve years ago, and there it was, the dress still hanging in its Laura Ashley bag, never to be worn again.

And then there was the champagne-colored shimmering silk dress I bought to wear to my son's wedding. The most gorgeous, expensive dress I had ever owned. I figured this would be the last wedding in the family, but it would also be the one and only time I would wear that dress.

Then there were the straight-legged tan trousers, three pairs all from Talbots "never to go out of style" I was told. All these, I had bought in a fit of madness because I loved the colors, or the style, and they suited me.

This summer though, because I had been through the trauma of down-sizing, this would be the year of clearing out. So quickly, before I had a chance to change my mind, I took all my treasures over to the Consignment Store.

Piece by piece she went through them, picking them over. "Too old", she said about my beautiful black evening dress, then the silk wedding dress she took, almost reluctantly; and marked it way down. The trousers were proclaimed "frumpy" "Talbots" I almost shrieked, so indignant was I "Classic". Nobody will buy them" she said "out of style". What happened to the "never go out of style" advice I received?

I reverently folded all my precious memories, all part of my life gone by, but now flung down and trodden into the dust, and I took them down to "Echo" where they were gratefully taken from my arms, and hung pride of place on their "Second Time Around" rack.

Now it gives me pleasure to think that somebody without much money will be able to wear with joy my long-cherished clothes that maybe aren't trendy, but classic and elegant, and never out of style.

It's Not All Bad Being Old!

There was a time
     when I could sit cross-legged
on the floor.
     There was a time
when I could stand on my head,
     and do high kicks,
and cartwheels,
     and high jumps,
and jitterbug,
     and run like the wind.

Now though, I am not so young.
     I cannot sit cross-legged
on the floor,
     because I can't get up again
without help.

     I cannot stand on my head,
nor do I want to
     see things upside down.

I don't walk so fast anymore
     but I do walk
I still dance in my kitchen
     when I hear Glenn Miller.

I have wrinkles yes.
     My arms have wrinkles too
and flap,
     and cheeks that sag
but that's alright.

I find I can smile at men
     and often do
without being called a flirt.
     It's not all bad being old.

Men say when I cross the road
     or walk on ice,
"Would you like an arm?"
     "Yes please" I say.

They also offer help
      to take my suitcase
off the carousel.
      "Thank you" I say
"that would be wonderful."

People come to help me
      clear my driveway.
"Thank you very much" I say
I don't even have to ask.

Best of all though
      I find now, that I can do
all the things I've loved
      and wanted all my life to do
and never had the time.

And so you see,
      it's not all bad, being old!

To the Gander

You grew out of water
you walk in mud
but your webbed feet
do not walk well in mud.

Your body is heavy
and your wings are strong
they will carry your body far away.

As a child you towered above me
your neck arched towards me.
I wanted to put my arms
around your strong shoulders
and nestle against you
bury my head in your soft feathers.
I wanted your wings to enfold me.
But you took the bread
from my small fingers
and moved away.
Even then though goose
I knew we were kin.

Beloved Gander
you are the other side of me
the "free to come and go" side
but I must stay here on the ground
where I belong
while you who share my soul.
will fly with the geese
in a long shimmering line.

You are the leader
bearing the brunt of the wind
while the geese in line behind you
fly in the lea of your strong wings
until another takes the lead
and you drop back.
But on and on you go
ever southward over mountains and plains
A compulsion that pulls you
South in the Fall
and North in the Spring.

154

My feet have wings
but I cannot fly.
You will have to do the flying
for both of us.

I hear you calling Gander
and one day I will come
I will nestle against your soft feathers
and become a part of you,
and you will show me the way.

Mountain High

To smell the warm sweet scent of pines,
    To leave the trees behind and feel the sun,
And walk through meadows thick with columbine.
    The path that winds and twists,
To climb it foot by foot with pounding heart,
    Always another crest to overcome.
To see the pin-small flowers in the grass,
    To turn the rocks that never saw the light
Until today.
    To hear the water bubbling down,
under, over, through.
    Emerging crystal clear, and icy cold
as the snow from whence it came.

To reach the last horizon,
    To stretch my arms,
And hold within my hands the mountain sky.
    And soar upon the wings of eagles.

Conclusion

Some of these were written as a collection of separate stories and published by *Serenity Magazine* of Evergreen, Colorado, which might explain the repeated phrases that crop up here and there.

I have decided that it isn't enough to have lived through those times. There aren't very many of us who are left who remember the depression, or "slump" as it was called in Britain, or World War II from an ordinary young person's point of view, and the long hard recuperative years.

I thought I ought to write them down, so I have.

There'll be more, I've no doubt, but this is all for now. Thank you for listening.

Jean Barringer was born in London, England, in 1926, and grew up during the blitz of World War II, spending most nights in a bomb shelter.

At the age of eighteen, she joined the British Women's Army, and spent three years as an army driver.

She married Anthony Barringer in 1948, and, after he graduated with a PhD from Royal School of Mines, emigrated to Canada in March 1954, with her 4-month-old baby, one month after her husband.

They lived in Toronto for six months, then transferred to New Brunswick for one year, and then to Ottawa for six months.

She and Anthony had four more children, all born in Canada. They came to Colorado in 1977, where she now lives.